Some People Think I Am Stupid

Some people think I am stupid.
Others think I don't care.
But to all of us who have dyslexia
Life seems totally unfair.

It doesn't matter how much I try
My hair is a mess, my shoes untied
My coat is undone, I spilt the tea
But at the end of the day I am still
only little old me.

I have to work much harder
to learn to read and write
but if you have this problem
don't give up without a fight.

Thank goodness there are people
who can help and understand
the plight of us dyslexics
because there are plenty of us around

Martyn Charity (11)

Dyslexics I Have Known

or

Reaching for the Stars

BEVÉ HORNSBY MBE, PhD, MEd, FRCSLT, AFBPsS, Hon FCP, FRSA, AMBDA

The Hornsby International Dyslexia Centre, London

Consultant in Dyslexia
PROFESSOR MARGARET SNOWLING
University of York

W
WHURR PUBLISHERS
LONDON AND PHILADELPHIA

© 2001 Whurr Publishers Ltd
First published 2001
by Whurr Publishers Ltd,
19b Compton Terrace
London N1 2UN, England and
325 Chestnut Street, Philadelphia PA 19106 USA

British Library Cataloguing in Publication Data
A catalogue record for this book is available from the British
Library.

ISBN 1 86156 197 0

Printed and bound in the UK by Athenaeum Press Ltd,
Gateshead, Tyne & Wear

Contents

Foreword

This book is part of a larger pattern. It shows what dyslexics can do once their problem is recognized and appropriate help provided. The thrust of the book is optimistic. The greatest sources of inspiration are faith and hope, and nothing stimulates these more powerfully than the example of what others have done. It is like a map of the possible. It links hope to reality and creates the faith that in turn fires effort.

The larger pattern is the shape of Bevé Hornsby's work in the field of dyslexia. Here in Cumbria, where I live, we have some good words for describing folk like Bevé. She's a 'bottomer', and she 'shapes up'. These may not sound elegant but they are extremely complimentary. A 'bottomer' is someone driven by a need to get to the bottom of things, whether practical or intellectual, an indispensable quality in pioneering research. All Bevé's early work aimed at two things, to get to the bottom of dyslexia through an empirical approach, analysing it by how it affected people, and to find out how far and by what methods dyslexics could be helped.

To 'shape up' is our northern way of saying that a person possesses initiative. The idea that initiative is simply the power to initiate action, to do something without having to be told, falls far short of the meaning that for us has built up around the phrase. A woman who 'shapes up' recognizes what needs to be done, feels it's up to her either to do it or get it done, finds out the best way to do it, organizes her energies, sets to work with zest and feels restless until the job is done. The job in this case was nothing less than to enlighten public opinion worldwide so that children suffering from dyslexia could be recognized, to train remedial teachers and, most difficult of all, to convert all existing teachers to her point of view.

Now Bevé has never claimed to be the first in the field, but she is nonetheless both unique and original. Her uniqueness was apparent in her early work as a speech therapist, in which she showed that she had the instincts of a true teacher, combining sympathetic insight into minds and feelings, an intuitive analytical power that enabled her to see the exact point

on which to work and how to approach it, a powerful creative urge that
inspired progress in her pupils and a gift for communication, not only of
fact or method, but of her whole self. Great teachers are rare but not
unique. To be an educational psychologist and a great teacher, on the other
hand, is unique. When she assesses a child she is at the same time working
out how she herself would set to work, and her judgement of how far a
given degree of dyslexia will affect the educational process is unerring.

Bevé's originality is of two kinds. First, the cast of her mind is original as
opposed to derivative. Her natural method is empirical. Those early years at
Bart's gave her the opportunity to observe case after case, to analyse, to
classify, to record and, on the basis of all that, to teach and to learn about
teaching by doing it. It is this first-hand element in her knowledge that gives
to her judgement its authority. Second, her originality may be seen in the
way she gives a lead. For instance, once she realized that dyslexics could be
helped and that teachers could be trained to help them, she set to work to
train them. Their success quickly became so palpable that others followed
her example. That is her way. She is a pathfinder.

Another instance concerns the use of the word 'dyslexia'. Her experiences at Bart's had convinced her early on that abnormal difficulty with
reading and writing were a part and not the whole, that they were
symptoms among other symptoms, such as poor concentration, poor short-
term memory, difficulty in perceiving sequence and so on, and that these
formed a varying syndrome of an underlying disorder in mental processing.
Others working in the field had reached the same perception. Difficulties
arose about the language used to express it. The word 'dyslexia' had been
coined as a label for difficulty with reading, writing and spelling. As understanding of the disorder deepened, the word seemed to many to be too
inaccurate, and psychologists began to replace it with the phrase 'specific
learning difficulties' (SLD). I telephoned one of them about an assessment
report he had sent me in which he had used the phrase. 'Is the boy
dyslexic?' I asked. 'That's a word we try not to use anymore', he replied.
'Then will you specify the specific difficulties?' He was reluctant at first: he
wasn't sure I'd understand him. Eventually he explained neatly enough
about the problems of short-term memory, inability to perceive order and
the rest. All he was doing was isolating certain symptoms in the dyslexic
syndrome.

Bevé would have none of this. Every good teacher has to be a popular-
izer. She knew instinctively that the fate of dyslexics lay ultimately in public
understanding, and that 'dyslexia' was an arresting word with a good
rhythm, a word easy in the mouth. She also knew that it is in the nature of
language for words to accumulate meaning, even to change meaning. It is
easy to cite examples of such etymological shifts. 'Cool', for instance, has

undergone several extensions. Beginning as 'fairly cold', it came to include 'calm', then 'unfriendly', then 'relaxed', then 'calmly daring' and finally the children of this generation use it for 'excellent'. Bevé knew that 'dyslexia' was the flag for the masthead, and that the public must be brought to understand that it stood for the underlying disorder and the varied combinations of symptoms. One of her assessment reports of that period reads, 'this girl certainly has a number of specific learning difficulties, sometimes called "dyslexia".' No wonder teachers love her! Here is the directness and clarity of true leadership.

When Bevé asked me to write this Foreword I felt very honoured. I also took it as a sign that my sins might have been expiated, for I was a very late convert. As Head of English in a major public school whose percentage pass mark in the Common Entrance Exam used to be high enough to sieve out dyslexics, I rarely came across them. I realize now that I occasionally did. Knowing nothing about dyslexia I treated them as lazy bums. I still burn with shame at the recollection. Then 22 years ago came illness, early retirement, recovery and my setting up as an independent private tutor for those needing help with O and A levels, and 'there' – to use Lear's words – 'I found 'em, there I smelt 'em out'. So I studied dyslexia. Pupil after pupil taught me more about it. To help them became an obsession. Then I made contact with Bevé Hornsby – and I have tried to live up to her standards.

David Alban
The Old Vicarage
Long Lane
Sedbergh
Cumbria

Preface

Children learn from their teachers, and teachers need tools. The tool most taken for granted is not only the most important, but the least understood – language. The patterns of our language are absorbed from birth but very few have an explicit knowledge of its phonetic and linguistic structure.

There are those who have a specific language learning difficulty who, for various reasons, do not internalize the sounds and patterns of their language. As a child grows this is often manifest in his or her school work, in the inability to use these structures and phonetic patterns, also often noticeable in speech patterns. This results in difficulty in reading, writing, spelling and written work, and the misunderstanding of the nuances of language. People who lack these essential skills cannot use language efficiently; this leads to failure, for in the modern world success is measured by the ability to pass written examinations, which mainly test linguistic skills. This particular difficulty has nothing to do with overall intelligence and is generally referred to as 'dyslexia'.

Professor Bevé Hornsby, from her experience as a speech therapist, clinician and not least a mother, saw the need for an uncomplicated textbook, which could be used by both teachers and parents to help explain explicitly what most people have internalized and cannot articulate. She devised a structured phonetic/linguistic programme, a clear concise guide to the English language in one volume. *Alpha to Omega* was thoroughly tested in the Dyslexia Clinic at St Bartholomew's Hospital before being published.

The present book is a follow-up of people taught using this system since its inception. It shows how defeat has been turned into success when a child's difficulties have been recognized. It also charts the difficulties and often the dire consequences where no help has been available.

Successive governments have been anxious to improve the standards of education in this country, so that the populace is literate and numerate, but until the basic problem of language, both written and spoken, is addressed, then all else is in vain. It is every child's birthright to be able to express himself or herself in both spoken and written language. Maths too will improve as all explanations use language, as do most of the questions.

The solving of literacy problems lies in our hands, if only people would listen. Basic techniques such as those set out in *Alpha to Omega* must form the core of our curriculum. These have to be presented many times in various interesting and humorous ways, encouraging children in the imaginative use of language. An adaptation of *Alpha to Omega* has been tried out in normal classrooms. This has proved very successful, eliminating much of the stress caused by unstructured spelling lists.

Teacher training colleges need to give explicit teaching in language, and training courses for the already qualified are also required.

There is much talk of setting up various organizations, such as pre-school play groups, after-school care and holiday groups. Anyone involved in such activities should have at least some rudimentary knowledge of language acquisition and structure so that they can recognize children's difficulties and refer them for help. The government and the authorities may feel this is a counsel of perfection, but should we not aim for this even though we may never reach it?

When Professor Hornsby wrote *Alpha to Omega* she could never have envisaged the impact it would make on so many lives, and for her work she was awarded the MBE.

Jean Baker
Former St Bartholomew's Hospital student
A severe dyslexic with two dyslexic sons

About the author

Bevé Hornsby is one of the pioneers of the dyslexia movement in the UK and was the first speech therapist to become seriously involved in the subject. She qualified as a speech therapist in 1969. Already very interested in language and its disorders, written as well as spoken, she obtained simultaneously part-time posts at a speech therapy clinic in Kingston, at St Thomas' Reading Difficulties Clinic and at the Word Blind Clinic at St Bartholomew's Hospital.

Two years later she became Head of the Word Blind Clinic and proceeded to expand this into the Dyslexia Department, with sponsorship from the Wolfson Foundation. One hundred and seventy patients were treated each week and the BBC made a programme based on the work of the Department, entitled 'I'm brighter than they think'.

In 1973, by popular demand, she started the first of the one-year teacher training courses for dyslexia therapists. This enabled hundreds of people to become trained to teach dyslexics and to enrich the knowledge of dyslexia by going on to become professors at universities and heads of some of the most famous schools for dyslexics in the country.

On retiring from Bart's, Dr Hornsby took the students enrolled on the course to Digby Stuart Training College and in 1984 started her own centre in Wandsworth.

Dr Hornsby's untiring dedication to the cause of the dyslexic's plight has helped hundreds of children and adults and enabled others to extend this good work throughout the English-speaking world.

She was honoured in the 1997 New Year Honours List for her work in this field and was made an MBE. In October 1997, she was made an Honorary Fellow of the College of Preceptors and she is also a Fellow of the Royal College of Speech and Language Therapists, a Fellow of the Royal Society of Arts and an Associate Fellow of the British Psychological Society. In November 1997, Dr Hornsby was given a Golden Award by the national charity Help the Aged for her pioneering work in the field of specific learning difficulties and later the same month became a professor at Cheltenham & Gloucester College of Higher Education.

There is now a flourishing Dyslexia Centre in Wandsworth, providing teacher training and spin-off, by teaching children in maintained schools and teaching reading to adults who have missed out on their earlier schooling. In 1988, Bevé started a prep school to demonstrate that the teaching philosophy she espoused regarding the acquisition of reading, writing and spelling skills was appropriate for all children; and that it could be used to create a template on which to base the teaching of literacy skills, enabling all children, whatever their abilities and disabilities, to learn. This has proved to be a correct hypothesis, as research has shown.

Publications

Alpha to Omega – the A–Z of teaching reading, writing and spelling. Oxford: Heinemann Educational.
The first of the multisensory teaching programmes to be published in the UK (in 1974), with numerous reprints and five new editions, the latest in 1999.
Alpha to Omega Flashcards. Oxford: Heinemann Educational.
First published in 1976, second edition in 1989, reprinted in 1990 and 1991.
Alpha to Omega Activity Packs 1 (1989), 2 (1993), 3 (1993) and One+ (1998).
A Walk Through Guide to Alpha to Omega (1996) London: The Hornsby Centre.
Overcoming Dyslexia: a straightforward guide for families and teachers. London: Random House.
First published in 1984 by Martin Dunitz. Reprinted in 1989, 1990, 1991. New editions 1992, 1995, 1996 and 1997.
Before Alpha: learning games for the under fives (1989) London: Souvenir Press. New edition 1996.

These books have changed both the attitude to dyslexia and the method of remediation over the past 26 years, influencing the change that is setting dyslexics free.

Author's Note

It is with great regret that I was not allowed to keep the names and addresses of all the children and adults who attended the Dyslexia Clinic at St Bartholomew's Hospital. The data from these patients were used for my PhD study, but once I had retired from Bart's my successor was reluctant to allow me access to the files, so addresses and original reports are not available, except for those with whom I have kept in contact.

These are the patients who are now grown up, in jobs, many of them married and with families. As a result there are only 14 of the original Bart's patients with whom I am in contact. However, since 1981, when I retired from Bart's and started my own assessment and teacher training centre, I have 120 subjects who have returned on a fairly regular basis for reassessment and examination concession certificates, advice on schools and careers, enough to make a study of their progress worthwhile. So I began to collect data purely for interest.

The objectives seemed to fall into the following categories:

- To what extent does the original assessment predict future achievement at school, in adult life?
- Do specific Wechsler Intelligence Scale for Children (WISC) profiles have any significance regarding progress in learning to read and write?
- To what extent has dyslexia proved to be a handicap or an advantage/ asset?

However, before I proceed any further I feel I should give some insight into the condition known as dyslexia and list some well-known definitions.

World Federation of Neurologists 1968

Specific developmental dyslexia 'A disorder manifested by difficulty in learning to read, despite conventional instruction, adequate intelligence and socio-cultural opportunity. It is dependent upon fundamental disabilities which are frequently of constitutional origin'.

Dyslexia 'A disorder in children, who despite conventional classroom experience fail to attain the language skills of reading, writing and spelling commensurate with their intellectual abilities'.

United States Congress

Learning disabilities 'Those children who have a disorder in one or more of the basic psychological processes involved in understanding or in using language, spoken or written, which disorder may manifest itself in imperfect ability to listen, think, speak, read, write, spell or do mathematical calculations. Such disorders include such conditions as perceptual handicaps, brain injury, minimal brain dysfunction, dyslexia, and developmental aphasia. Such a term does not include children who have learning problems which are primarily the result of visual, hearing or motor handicaps, or mental retardation, of emotional disturbance or environmental, cultural or economic disadvantage'.

MacDonald Critchley 1978

Developmental dyslexia 'A learning disability which initially shows itself by difficulty in learning to read, and later by erratic spelling and by a lack of facility in manipulating written as opposed to spoken words. The condition is cognitive in essence, and usually genetically determined. It is not due to intellectual inadequacy or to lack of socio-cultural opportunity, or to faults in the techniques of teaching, or to emotional factors, or to any known structural brain defect. It probably represents a specific maturational defect which tends to lessen as the child gets older, and is capable of considerable improvement, especially when appropriate remedial help is offered at the earliest opportunity.

I do, of course, investigate other signs and symptoms more fully in later chapters, but as far as I am concerned I consider the disparity between an individual's intellectual level and that of his or her academic achievement to be the crucial diagnostic indicator – although there are those who would disagree with me.

Being originally a speech and language therapist does tend to colour my attitude to dyslexia and the importance I give to speech and language development in its remediation.

I begin, therefore, by looking into the question of intelligence and the role it plays in the diagnostic procedures.

Margaret Rawson, in her excellent book *Developmental Language Disability: adult accomplishments of dyslexic boys* (1968) poses the hypothesis that 'Given average or better intelligence, physical normality and equivalent social and educational opportunity in both groups, differences in educational and vocational achievement by adulthood on the part of non-dyslexic boys and dyslexic boys, so diagnosed between the ages of six and twelve, will not be greater than could be explained by chance alone.'

She quotes the 'clinical hypothesis', which maintains the opposite, namely, 'dyslexic students, so diagnosed between the ages of six and twelve necessarily have substantially poorer prospects than do non-dyslexic students for success in later educational and occupational achievement'.

This study hopes to show that it is not only the question of being dyslexic or non-dyslexic that lies at the root of the question concerning further achievement, but also the quality of the initial assessment and the subsequent help provided.

Clearly I cannot quote every life story individually, so much of the information will be presented in the form of statistical figures and tables giving averages. Individual differences are inevitably lost using this method, so only cases where the principle is clearly defined will be given in full.

Of course, all the dyslexics assessed at the centre have subsequently had help of one sort or another with varying degrees of success. To provide a control group to form a contrast (if any) in achievement, both in relation to school and the workplace, I requested a chapter (Chapter 11) from someone engaged in counselling dyslexic adults, namely Jean Jones of the Wirral Dyslexia Association. I am sorry to report that Jean died in April 2000.

Nevertheless, of the 130 dyslexics who have agreed to be included in this study, 98 are 17 or more years of age, so it is possible to follow them into adult life.

Bevé Hornsby

References

Critchley M, Critchley EA (1978) *Dyslexia Defined.* London: Heinemann Medical.
Rawson M (1968) *Developmental Language Disability: adult accomplishments of dyslexic boys.* Baltimore: Johns Hopkins Press.

CHAPTER 1

The nature of intelligence

First we should perhaps discuss what we mean by intelligence. Although intelligence has been understood to describe something real and measurable and is as ancient as mankind itself, over the past 30 years it has become a pariah in the world of ideas. This would seem to have come about as a result of the move from the left to insist on equality no matter how much people differ from one another in every respect, including intelligence.

Charles Darwin's theory of evolution stimulated the scientific interest in the question of intelligence and its heritability. Sir Francis Galton, Darwin's young cousin, seized on this idea and set out to demonstrate its continuing relevance by using the great families of Britain as a primary source of data. He presented the evidence in his book *Hereditary Genius* published in 1869, just one decade after Darwin's *Origin of Species* in 1859. So began a long and deeply controversial association between intelligence and heredity that remains with us today.

Galton's tests were not very successful, but in 1870, Alfred Binet developed tests that were much less crude and led to the concept of mental age. In 1904, a British Army Officer named Charles Spearman made a statistical breakthrough which has shaped the development of mental tests ever since. He discovered the correlation coefficient which enabled the relationship between two variables to be measured on a scale ranging from -1 to $+1$.

A positive correlation means the degree to which one phenomenon is linked to another. Height and weight, for example, have a positive correlation (the taller, the heavier, for example). A positive correlation is one that falls between zero and $+1$, with $+1$ being an absolute reliable, linear relationship. A negative correlation falls between 0 and -1, with -1 also representing an absolutely reliable, linear relationship, but in the inverse direction. A correlation of 0 means no linear relationship whatsoever. Reading ability and intelligence are usually relatively highly correlated at around 0.6, which is why an IQ test is crucial in testing for reading failure since this relationship is often missing. In other words, the subject may be highly intelligent and yet still be unable to learn to read and write. Hence the term 'SPECIFIC learning difficulty/dyslexia', which identifies the learning difficulty relative to expectation based on the intellectual level.

Why are most correlations positive? Because they tap into the general trait. Spearman's statistical method is now known as factor analysis. He called this universal trait 'g' for general intelligence. This 'g' was defined as a person's capacity for complex mental work. By 1917 the concept of IQ rather than mental age was generally accepted and used by the US Army to classify recruits for the First World War.

In 1922–23, Lewis Terman, the developer of the Stanford–Binet IQ test (Terman 1916), was criticized by Lippmann for imposing superiority or inferiority on an individual in 50 minutes, but nevertheless, that is what we do and it is surprisingly accurate.

The vindication of Sir Cyril Burt, accused of fraudulently falsifying data on his study of twins who were reared apart but produced an IQ coefficient of +0.77, was realized in 1990, when the Minnesota twin study found the correlation to be +0.78, which showed that Burt's contention that intelligence is largely inherited is probably true (Mackingtosh 1995). IQs are usually, but not invariably, constant throughout a person's life, but can be affected by environmental factors as Gould (1981) pointed out.

Jean Piaget lived at the same time as Binet, and both have played a significant part in the development of the modern-day IQ (Piaget 1952). Of course, talents and intelligence describe different things, as do qualities – charm, sensitivity, insight, etc. – but it is often possible to identify aptitudes from the results on a test such as the Wechsler Intelligence Scale for Children (WISC) (1949), the Wechsler Adult Intelligence Scale (WAIS) or the Wechsler Pre-School and Primary Intelligence Scale.

One cannot necessarily identify intelligence with attractive human qualities, so this thing we know as IQ is important, but not as a synonym for human excellence nor for whether a person with a high IQ is likely to be someone you are going to like, admire or cherish. Indeed, quite the reverse in many cases. Herrstein & Murray in their book, *The Bell Curve* (1994) have identified the following facts.

- There is such a thing as a general factor of cognitive ability on which human beings differ.
- All standardized tests of academic aptitude or achievement measure this general factor to some degree, but IQ tests expressly designed for that purpose measure it more accurately.
- IQ scores match to a first degree, whatever it is that people mean when they use the words intelligent or smart in ordinary language.

- IQ scores are stable, although not perfectly so, over much of a person's life.
- Properly administered IQ tests are not demonstrably biased against social, economic, ethnic or racial groups.
- Cognitive ability is substantially heritable, apparently no less than 40% and no more than 80%.

Turning to the question of whether I, personally, tend to give a higher IQ than other psychologists, as one headmaster once said in a fit of irritation is, of course, strictly speaking not possible, since all the questions that you have to ask, and similarly the responses that you are allowed to score, are laid down in the manual. This accusation regarding my results being higher than those of other psychologists is fundamentally nonsense.

However, there are clearly factors that do affect a child's response to testing. I remember once employing an educational psychologist at the Centre who took three children in her first week, all of whom she reduced to either tears or vomiting. Clearly she was not getting the best out of the child, which is the aim of the test, as David Wechsler maintains in all his introductions to IQ testing. It is not surprising, therefore, that she did not last longer than a week!

Similarly, people who have strong accents, either dialectal or Hyper-RP (RP means received pronunciation, Queen's English or, in more modern terminology, educated London), affect comprehension. My predecessor at Bart's, Maisie Holt, when giving a test to an East London child, gave a perfect example of how pronunciation affects understanding, when she was asking him the vocabulary questions, the first of which is 'What is a hat?' Unfortunately, she always pronounced it 'het' and the child repeated it saying, 'Et, I don't know what et is, never 'eard of et.' Of course I couldn't resist interrupting to say, 'Hat child, hat.' 'Oh 'at, what you put on your 'ed, eh?' I don't think Maisie ever forgave me for that!

Certainly strong accents do affect comprehension, which is why in the good old days we always had people with RP accents talking on the BBC because anyone can understand a speaker with an educated accent, which is not true of heavy Scottish, Irish, Welsh or indeed, American accents. Apparently, Australian and South African English are nearer to Standard English than any of the aforementioned.

However, there are other factors as well that may affect a child's response to testing. One is a pleasant environment to come into, a friendly reception both by whoever answers the door and takes them to the waiting room and by the psychologist himself/herself. To put a child at ease is one of the first prerequisites of all testing situations, and the examiner is not barred from having a chat between sections of the test to find out what the child likes or dislikes about life and what he or she is finding difficult at home or at school. It will also aid diagnosis and the help that can be provided if the examiner has some idea of the child's background problems.

As we noted from the questionnaires that were sent out to parents, the general consensus was very favourable regarding the assessment and the effects it had on the child, the parents and the school. The attitude of the child to his problem and the motivation he brought to his work once he realized that it was possible to learn to read and write changed almost immediately. And, of course, the attitude of the parents to the child also changed when they realized that it is no good getting cross and nagging when what the child needs is help and encouragement, not criticism. The change of attitude of schools to the child's problem is, I am sorry to say, variable, ranging from very helpful to total disregard of the problem. However, it is interesting to note that one questionnaire filled out anonymously by one of our clients maintained that virtually nothing was helpful!

Inevitably the quality of psychologists engaged in assessments varies as it does in any profession. There will be those who are better at putting the child at ease and, therefore, obtaining a more satisfactory result than others who are somewhat intimidating. I also feel that it is advantageous for the child to come to another environment to be tested rather than being tested at school, where everything tends to be rather frightening, especially being called out of class and probably being tested in the headmaster's study, which is not conducive to a relaxed atmosphere. Also, a discussion with the parents at the time of the assessment is not possible so no background history of early development can be obtained.

Although I firmly believe that the WISC is by far the most reliable, and tests virtually every aspect of intelligence that can be tested, there are other characteristics of a personality which one cannot test and these will undoubtedly affect his or her success in life. We all know of the highly intelligent professor who is totally incapable of organizing his life in an intelligent fashion and goes to meetings improperly dressed or cannot find the relevant papers because he has no idea how to file things accurately.

David Wechsler himself stresses the importance of the administration environment, saying that the competent examiner has his materials properly organized, has a quiet friendly room, establishes a friendly relationship between himself and the subject, and allows sufficient time for the test to be administered in an easy manner, satisfying to both the examiner and the subject. Since children often react unfavourably to test procedures that imply concealment from them, it is better to arrange the table and chairs, box of materials – the whole setting – in a straightforward manner, which implies that a friendly, co-operative experience is about to take place. Calm movements and easy conversation by the examiner can do much to relieve any uncertainty and tension that the child may feel on being subjected to a test.

When I was working at Bart's we had, by chance, the ideal chairs and tables for testing hyperactive children. The legs of both the tables and the chairs had rubber tips, and the chairs had arms that fitted exactly under the table. When the child arrived and was invited to sit down – 'Come along Johnny, you sit here in the comfortable chair' – he was pushed in and became a virtual prisoner, escape being almost impossible. Of course, action was immediately necessary to maintain his enforced attention and activities changed the moment that attention showed signs of wandering. It worked like a dream!

It was not always understood by parents that Bart's, being a teaching hospital, invariably had students observing, whether one was testing or teaching. I was so thrilled by the success I was having with one 6-year-old, who had never been known to sit still for two seconds together and now concentrated for a full 40 minutes, that I invited the visual aids department to come and video the session. This, too, was highly successful as the child paid no attention to the cameras or to the constant ringing of the telephone and just carried on with his lesson as before.

Tommy during videoed lesson.

However, his mother must have complained to the father that I was making an exhibition of their child and the following week when we were in the middle of our lesson an obviously irate gentleman burst into the room. I arose, holding out my hand in greeting exclaiming, 'Mr Drummond, I presume', upon which the small child looked up and said, 'Are you going to kiss her Daddy?' This was not what he had in mind, but it deflated whatever it was he intended to say and he felt obliged to take a seat and observe the rest of the lesson. Sadly, they withdrew the child from treatment, and I often wonder what happened to him.

References

Darwin C (1859) *The Origin of Species by means of Natural Selection*. London: Murray

Galton F. (1869) *Hereditary Genius: an inquiry into laws of consequences*. London: Macmillan.

Gould SJ (1981) *The Mismeasure of Man*. New York: WW Norton. Also (1977) *Ever Since Darwin: reflections in natural history*. New York: WW Norton.

Herrstein RJ, Murray C (1994) *The Bell Curve*. New York: The Free Press.

Mackingtosh NJ (ed) (1995) *Cyril Burt; fraud or framed*. Oxford: Oxford University Press.

Piaget J (1952) *The Origins of Intelligence in Children*. Translated by M Cook. New York: International Universities Press.

Spearman C (1904, 1927) *The Abilities of Man*. New York & London: Macmillan.

Terman LM (1916) *The Measurement of Intelligence*. Boston, MA: Houghton Mifflin.

Wechsler D (1949) *Wechsler Intelligence Scale for Children*. New York: The Psychological Corporation.

CHAPTER 2

Is it possible for IQ results to differ?

Do IQs differ when tests are given by different psychologists? Strictly speaking, this should never happen, given the standard error of measurement, as the procedures are standardized, but there are occasions when they have differed. Sometimes a slightly lower result has been obtained relative to those derived previously. But when slightly higher IQs have resulted, they have been fully vindicated by future achievements, as the following case histories will show.

Factors affecting IQ testing

David Wechsler, in his manual of instructions (1939), has unequivocally stated that the object is to obtain the best possible result from the subject being tested.

To achieve this, he recommends that the testing room should be light, airy, warm and inviting, and that the furniture should be of a suitable size and arrangement to make both the examiner and the subject thoroughly comfortable and at ease. This will enable free manipulation of the materials and make the recording of responses easy and accurate. These conditions, needless to say, are not always observed.

Sufficient time should be allowed to enable a good rapport to be established and to allow some interchange of a conversational nature to take place between tests. Appropriate types of remarks, such as 'Good!', 'Well, that didn't take you long' or 'I think you will enjoy this one', are permitted and should be used to encourage and maintain interest, without indicating directly whether the response was correct or not.

Directions and questions, Wechsler states, should be read clearly and distinctly. A subject's failure to understand them should never be due to the examiner's poor or deviant enunciation!

In most of the oral tests, where scoring is inevitably more subjective, the examiner is allowed to ask the subject to explain more fully if a response is incomplete or unclear and this technique, known as 'questioning', may improve both scoring accuracy and qualitative understanding of the responses. However, it imposes on the examiner the responsibility for being thoroughly familiar with scoring criteria and for employing such querying skilfully. Long experience and an intuitive insight into the subject's possible potential are essential features of the finer details involved in such testing.

Some psychologists have an uncanny gift for diagnosing and detecting problems that other psychologists have often missed – particularly involving hearing, vision and language development. This may, of course, be due to their background training, which can bring to the testing situation skills and training that other psychologists lack. This probably stems from the fact that some psychologists are also speech therapists as well as clinical psychologists, which makes them more aware of, and knowledgeable about, matters affecting the sense organs and their neurological correlates.

At the Hornsby Centre great care is taken to ensure that clients are greeted by a sympathetic and welcoming secretary/receptionist, that the surroundings are as attractive and non-threatening as possible, and that visitors' comfort is catered for by offering refreshments, toilet facilities and a pleasant waiting room with magazines for the adults and suitable toys for the children. The consulting room is a delight, with charming views of gardens and trees.

There are four psychologists working at the Centre and, as far as is known, no one has ever felt threatened by the testing situation; indeed, many seem to thoroughly enjoy themselves.

All this undoubtedly contributes to creating the right frame of mind in which both children and adults can give of their best. It is interesting to note that when reassessment has been conducted by a psychologist other than the one who originally assessed the client, the results have been very similar, which could suggest that the surroundings are of equal importance to the tester's skill and manner.

It must also be remembered that a given score on a given day is not necessarily immutable. This is why confidence intervals are quoted, within which it can be reliably stated that the individual's score will fall, no matter how many times the same test is given, provided the interval between testing is more than two years to avoid any possible practice effect.

I quote three typical case studies where original IQs given by other psychologists have eventually proved to be underestimations of true potential, as their subsequent achievements bear witness.

Case study 1: Denis

Denis originally appeared as a case study in my book *Overcoming Dyslexia*. He was the first patient I was given to teach at Bart's Hospital Word Blind

Clinic in 1969 and was assessed by my predecessor, Maisie Holt. Denis was a total non-starter as far as reading and writing were concerned and his IQ was as follows:

- verbal IQ: 109
- performance IQ: 92
- full-scale IQ: 101

where 100 is average.

He exhibited all the classic dyslexic signs and symptoms, being left-handed but right-eyed, was dyspraxic (a clumsy child) and was very late on speech and language development. Denis reacted badly to his failure to learn and developed behaviour problems so he was sent to a school for maladjusted children, which did him no good at all. By the time he found his way to Bart's at the age of 10, his family had returned him to a normal middle school in Wimbledon, who were very sympathetic.

Eventually it became clear that Denis was highly intelligent and at the age of 15 a further IQ test was administered in which he obtained a full-scale IQ of 130, which placed him in the very superior range of intellectual ability (see Appendix 3).

At 16 Denis passed O levels in English literature, English language, geography, history, biology, chemistry, mathematics and social studies. Two years later he passed A levels in economics and geography, and went on to get a degree in geography. He now works as an executive civil servant.

It was not thought that his dyslexia was inherited but he now has two children, a boy and a girl, and the boy is severely dyslexic.

Case study 2: Charles

The second example of underestimated potential is Charles Flodin (born 29 January 1981), who was originally seen at a hospital clinic at the age of 7. The WISC was administered, with the following results:

- verbal IQ: 103
- performance IQ: 117
- full-scale IQ: 110

I saw Charles on 3 February 1988 to clarify the question of dyslexia and suggest suitable treatment, as he was a total non-starter and could not even write his own name. I recommended Mrs Pamela Morley, who trained at Bart's, and on reassessment on 18 December 1991, at the age of 10 years 10 months, Charles's improvement was so dramatic that I felt the first IQ assessment must have been an underestimation. Charles could now read to the 9 year 9 month level for accuracy and 11 years 2 months for comprehension. His spelling was at the 9-year level. I, therefore, gave the Raven's Coloured Progressive Matrices and Crichton Vocabulary Scale on which he performed at grade one, above the 95th percentile, placing him in the very superior range of intellectual ability. Subsequent achievements have vindicated this finding as Charles obtained three As and six Bs in his GCSEs and is predicted three As at A level. It was only on my letter of recommendation that St Dunstan's College was prepared to accept him and he has done them proud.

Case study 3: Ewan

A third example of incorrect predictions was Ewan. He was referred to the Hornsby Centre by his GP in Gerrards Cross, who suspected Ewan was dyslexic but was not receiving any specialist help.

He was assessed by Mr John Walker, one of the educational psychologists at the Centre, on 9 September 1987, at the age of 8 years 9 months. Ewan was found to have a verbal IQ of 137, a performance IQ of 121 and a full-scale IQ of 132, which placed him in the very superior range of intellectual ability.

In spite of this, the school insisted that Ewan was average and unlikely to achieve much! However, his mother wrote to tell us that *Alpha to Omega* (Hornsby et al. 1999) had 'saved his bacon' and he achieved nine GCSEs and four A levels at the following grades: chemistry A, physics A, electronics B and maths B. Ewan is now going to York University and was chosen first out of six candidates for scholarship.

References

Hornsby B, Shear F (1999) *Alpha to Omega – the A–Z of teaching reading, writing and spelling*, 5th edn. Oxford: Heinemann Educational.

Wechsler D (1939) *Wechsler Bellevue Intelligence Scale*. New York: The Psychological Corporation.

CHAPTER 3

Diagnostic procedures

Of course, there are other aspects to a diagnosis apart from IQ testing, but it is the disparity between what one should expect regarding achievement relative to cognitive functioning that gives the clue to something being amiss.

Next come reading and spelling tests and a timed passage of free writing, which often uncovers typical errors and omissions not present in the spelling test, and discloses flaws in handwriting and positioning of the paper, head or body.

If the child is a total non-starter it is necessary to test for 'knowledge of the alphabet' (see page 14 in *Alpha to Omega*, Hornsby et al. 1999).

It should be automatic that vision and hearing are, or have recently been, investigated, and careful note should be made of the child's behaviour and ability to concentrate.

Similarly, a detailed case history, including family history and the patient's early history, is imperative. I always test for handedness and eyedness, and find the Bangor Dyslexia Test useful here as it also incorporates sequencing and memory tests. Of course, not all crossed laterals are dyslexic, but I have noticed that if written language is not affected, their consciousness of themselves in space is often faulty. They also tend to make appalling car drivers, because they are unable to judge the speed at which cars are approaching or the speed with which they, themselves, are approaching the vehicles in front. White knuckles for the passenger!

There is a growing proliferation of overlapping conditions, often accompanied by supplementary treatments heralded as 'cures' by the practitioners. If these are wildly expensive they should be treated with caution, since nothing can supplant good teaching, it can only complement it.

Among these conditions are the following:

- attention deficit disorder, with or without hyperactivity
- neurodevelopmental delay

- scotopic sensitivity – involving coloured spectacles or contact lenses
- dietary supplementation
- allergies
- cranial osteopathy
- music therapy
- movement therapy
- sound therapy
- neurolinguistic programming

and so on.

In some cases some of these are appropriate, but I doubt they are magic cures. Still, the proof of trying is in the succeeding, and if the child cannot learn the way you teach, teach the way he learns.

Of course, it will be necessary to check for the following diagnostic signs and symptoms of the dyslexic syndrome, although they will not necessarily all be present.

Signs and symptoms of specific learning difficulties (SLD)

- difficulty with literacy skills and sometimes some aspects of numeracy
- short-term memory weaknesses – auditory and/or visual.
- auditory and/or visual perception difficulties
- language difficulties
- sequencing difficulties
- left/right confusion
- mixed dominance
- motor problems
- reversal of letters and words
- short attention span
- disorganization
- erratic performance
- hyperactivity.

The pre-school child will have a different set of at-risk factors to take into consideration.

Identifying the pre-schooler 'at risk' for SLD

Remember: children develop at different rates. Each child must be treated as an individual and all aspects of their development must be considered.

- Difficulty in pinpointing the 'at-risk' child.

- Learning to be aware of how the child is functioning within his/her environment.
- Hearing:
  - sensorineural hearing loss
  - glue ear
  - poor attention development.
- Vision:
  - acuity
  - squint
  - convergence
  - light sensitivity.
- Motor development:
  - gross
  - fine.
- Attention:
  - delayed/appropriate.
- Play:
  - delayed/appropriate.
  - Speech and language development:
  - comprehension/expression.
- Social/emotional development.

Of course, there is now a proliferation of supplementary, complementary and even alternative treatments coming on to the market on an almost daily basis.

Buzan books

The Tony Buzan books, published by the BBC, have had a considerable influence on study skills and memory techniques. There are now a number of Buzan Centres around the country (more information from Vanda North, Managing Director, 54 Parkstone Road, Poole, Dorset BH15 2PX). The first of the Buzan books was published in 1972 and they have various titles such as *Use Your Head*, *Use your Memory* and *Speed Reading*, all of which are intended to 'make the most of your mind'.

'Look up and remember'

This was devised by Alan Heath as exercises to help children remember spelling patterns (O'Connor & Seymour 1990). Relaxation methods are used to complement the brain's functions and activate the visual. There are now many practitioners and they concentrate on a visual approach to develop a strategy for spelling as opposed to an auditory one; this is often linked to neurolinguistic programming.

The Tomatis method

The Tomatis method was developed over 20 years ago by Professor Tomatis in Paris. His premiss was that some children were unable to block out environmental noise to concentrate on what the teacher was saying. This is often not detected by an ordinary hearing test. Unfortunately, the treatment is very expensive and time consuming and involves retraining the hearing apparatus by listening to music played through special headphones. It would appear to be very similar to that offered by sound therapy clinics. The centre started by Patrick de la Roque is at: The Alfred A Tomatis Foundation (Lewis) Ltd, 3 Wellands Crescent, Lewis, East Sussex BNY 2QT.

Reflexology

Reflexology has been offered as a cure for almost any and every ailment. There are claims that it relieves the frustration that many dyslexics feel as it works on the brain and spinal cord, stimulating nerve endings and improving the memory by bringing more oxygen to the brain. There are innumerable reflexologists working around the country. The International Federation of Reflexologists, 76–78 Edridge Rd, Croydon CRO 1EF will be able to find one in your area.

Cranial osteopathy

Cranial osteopathy has proved helpful in a number of cases. As Stuart North says, 'Anything which causes the baby to be out of alignment can upset his or her spatial awareness and, therefore, learning. The brain has its own movement and if it is not moving in a balanced fashion, that can also hinder the learning ability of the child.' The address for further information is: The Osteopathic Centre for Children, 19a Cavendish Square, London W1M 9AD.

Neurophysiological psychology

It was AE Tansly's comment over 20 years ago that far too many teachers concentrated on emotional problems and socioeconomic environments to account for children's literacy problems that led Peter Blythe to set up the Institute of Neuro-Physiological Psychology in Chester to search for a physical basis for learning difficulties. He found that primitive and postural reflexes that should have disappeared in the maturation of the nervous system had failed to do so, and corrective exercises were necessary to put this right before the child could be said to be ready to cope with his or her learning difficulties. The address is: The Institute of Neuro-Physiological

Psychology, 4 Stanley Place, Chester CHI 2LU. A book is also available, *A Teacher's Window into the Child's Mind* (published by Fern Ridge Press, 1927 Mclean Boulevarde, Engen, OR 97405, USA).

Coloured lenses and contact lenses

There is much controversy over the effectiveness of coloured overlays or lenses to prevent words from moving about on the page, and when Helen Irlen first offered these spectacles in 1983, to both adults and children, she was criticized for being a charlatan without scientific back-up. There is still some lack of understanding as to why they appear to work for some people, but there are suggestions that the mago cells in the eyes (the large cells that detect fast movement) work more sluggishly in dyslexics so that the parvo cells, which detect small detail and colour, are not functioning in unison. It seems that pale blue works best.

Dr Tallal maintains that a parallel slowness in detecting fine differences in sounds also exists in dyslexics and maintains that if 'b' and 'd' are slowed down the difference between /ba/ and /da/ can be detected. However, /b/ and /d/ are plosives, and the sound is only perceived when the air is released – in this case on the /a/. Thus all she is doing is extending the vowel 'ah' and that cannot help differentiation between /b/ and /d/.

Ah well, no doubt all will one day be explained.

Nutrition and diet

Many dyslexics have allergies and these need investigating. However, some impressive research has been conducted by Dr Jacqueline Stordy of Efamol Ltd into a unique supplement called Efalex, available in capsule form. Efalex has five live ingredients designed to maximize the incorporation of essential fatty acids into the eye and the brain. Eight capsules a day, taken for at least three months, are needed for any benefit to be noticeable.

ADD, with or without hyperactivity

The Centre Academy, 92 St John's Hill, London SW11 1SH is the UK branch of the American Centre, and its practitioners are considered the experts on this condition. However, it is unclear as to whether the attention deficit is due to a receptive language disorder, which is difficult to assess, or to some brain dysfunction. True hyperactivity, once known as hyperkinetic syndrome, is definitely a defect in the inhibitors in the brain, which cannot repress the inappropriate behaviour these children exhibit. The treatment offered is usually in the form of drugs, particularly Ritalin, which do have side effects. In the UK, we prefer to try homeopathic and behaviour modification remedies before resorting to drugs.

The Sunflower method

Mark Matthews is responsible for starting the Sunflower method at the Reve Pavilion, 2a Guildford Park, Guildford, Surrey GU2 5ND. This method incorporates virtually all the methods already mentioned in the one setting. Thus, it uses homeopathic remedies, massage and osteopathy to cure neurological imbalances that lead to learning difficulties, but often elude mainstream practitioners. The results of this holistic approach are felt by some to be startlingly successful. Mark Matthews himself is dyslexic and is an applied kinesiologist.

Kumon maths

Since numbers can often be a problem in dyslexia, I feel I should mention the Kumon maths approach, since it is so similar to *Alpha to Omega* in its approach. In other words, it progresses in small steps in a structured and very organized way. A child studying in this way will gain confidence by not being asked to do anything he or she has not understood, and each step builds on the one that went before.

Recommended reading

Carter R (1998) *Mapping the Mind.* London: Weidenfeld & Nicolson. Paperback edition 1999 published by Orion.

Hornsby B (1997) *Overcoming Dyslexia: a straightforward guide for families and teachers*, revised edn. London: Random House.

Hornsby B (1996) *Before Alpha: learning games for the under fives*, revised edn. London: Souvenir Press.

Hornsby B, Shear F, Pool J (1999) *Alpha to Omega – the A–Z of teaching reading, writing and spelling,* 5th edn. Oxford: Heinemann Educational.

Miles TR (1983) *The Bangor Dyslexia Test.* Wisbech: Learning Development Aids.

Miles TR (1993) *The Pattern of Difficulties.* London: Whurr.

Miles TR (2000) *Music and Dyslexia.* London: Whurr.

References for alternative treatments

British Society for Nutritional Medicine, Dr Alan Stewart, 5 Somerhill Road, Hove, East Sussex BN3 IRP.

Buzan T (1989) *Use your Head* (and other titles). London: BBC Books. There are now many Buzan Centres around the country which claim to 'make the most of your mind'. For more information contact Vanda North, Managing Director, 54 Parkstone Road, Poole, Dorset BH15 2PX.

Holland K, Tyrell R, Wilkins A (1991) The effect of Irlen coloured lenses on saccadic eye movements and reading. *Applied Vision Assoicates* **20**: 7.

Kibel M (1995) *Sound Works*. Jolly Learning. Unfortunately, the scheme is very expensive and teaches only 26 letter sounds and no names. It has been adopted by City and Guilds as the educational material in their accreditation course for assistant teachers in state schools.

Kumon Maths, Kumon Educational UK, Ground Floor, Elscot House, Arcadia Avenue, London N3 2JU.

O'Connor J, Seymour J (1990) *Introducing Neurolinguistic Programming*. London: HarperCollins.

The Sound Learning Centre, 12 The Rise, London N13 5LE. Also teaches auditory integration training, lightwave stimulation, instrumental enrichment, neurodevelopmental delay.

CHAPTER 4

Dyslexia as a language disorder

Language disorders can be very subtle, particularly where comprehension is concerned, and this disability is not always understood by educational psychologists because their training does not normally include an in-depth study of language.

Language has been shown to be biological and innate, as we are born with a language acquisition device (LAD), an area of the brain, usually in the left hemisphere, which is specifically geared to the comprehension and production of speech and language.

The two things are not necessarily synonymous, as it is possible to have speech without language, if by language one understands 'meaningful communication', and language without speech.

A child with hydrocephalus (water on the brain) may produce a stream of speech sounds or words which have little, if any, meaning. Similarly, it is a mistake to assume that if speech is not present, there can be no inner language development. The totally deaf child, who may never develop speech, nearly always shows evidence of the presence of language and usually learns to read and write. The cerebral palsy sufferer who cannot talk may turn out to be a brilliant author, like Christy Brown, who could control no muscles in his body except those in his left foot yet produced three novels and three volumes of verse by typing with his left foot before he died at the age of 49.

The way into an aphasic child's language area is often through the written word, since he or she is unable to make sense of the spoken word. We are talking, of course, about the developmental aphasic who is born with a defective language area, not the acquired aphasic who has suffered brain damage as the result of a stroke or an accident of some kind.

However, returning to the individual whose muscle control is normal and whose sense organs are in working order, all that is necessary for language to develop is that he or she be exposed to it. The only human of this kind known to have no language as we understand it, is feral man, the most talked about being the wild boy of Avalon, who was reared by wolves. Even then it was felt that he could also have been autistic, because he never developed speech even when found and returned to civilization.

Lenneberg, in his book *The Biological Foundations of Language* (1967), maintains that the critical period for acquiring spoken language is from 0 to 5 and the critical period for acquiring written language is from 5 to 15. Of course, these skills can still be mastered after these ages, but the mastering will be that much more difficult and that much more inefficient. This is because the young brain cells are able to change and adapt their function more easily. As the brain matures this plasticity becomes less and eventually the function of the cells becomes fixed. This does not mean that we cannot learn after a certain age, but it means that if some groups of cells are functioning inefficiently other groups cannot take over their job. The only thing that can be done is to find a way to circumvent the difficulty.

Language development begins from birth, of course, with the baby becoming aware of the sound of his or her mother's voice and the soothing and comforting effect this should have. The baby's own output begins to have meaning too, so that the cries become differentiated into those of hunger, pain or anger. At three months babbling is in full swing, with other noises appearing, such as gurgles, burps, coos, sighs, blowing raspberries with bilabial voiced fricatives. In fact, the infant's babble contains every sound that might be required for whatever language he or she is eventually going to produce. Babble is universal. By six months the baby is also imitating himself or herself and indulging in vocal play and it will be noticed that intonation patterns have begun to sound something like German, French, English, Italian, Welsh, Scottish or whatever.

Between 6 and 9 months the baby begins to imitate others when they babble at him or her, and comprehension is starting. The baby recognizes his or her own name and usually understands the word 'No'. This is often the first word that is produced, rather than Daddy and Mummy. By the age of one, the baby should say his or her first words with meaning. Babbling or jargon carries on, with up to 20 words mixed in, but there is usually a plateau between 15 months and 18 months while walking becomes firmly established. Once that is mastered and becomes automatic, speech goes ahead again and by the age of two there should be up to 200 words and short phrases, by three up to 900 words and talking in full sentences. Some consonantal substitutions may be present, but speech should be intelligible. By the age of four, language should be complete except, possibly, some immature grammar such as: 'I runned', 'me want it'.

This is the great question period. It is believed that the quality of the answers parents give at this time determines whether a child develops an elaborated or a restricted code and affects cognitive development. Middle-

and upper-class families are supposed to produce children with an elaborated code and working-class with a restricted code. This of course, as with everything, is only part of the truth, otherwise how could great brains, great thinkers, great artists, great writers, be able to come from working-class backgrounds?

Children can be deprived from any social background. Good language development springs more from the expansion of the child's utterances rather than anything else. For example:

- Child: 'Daddy gone?'
- Mother: 'Yes, Daddy has gone to work, but he will be back at supper time.'

There must obviously be some truth in the background, or class, theory, which explains why so many middle-class children develop better language and on the whole earlier reading skills than working-class children. But again, it is not the whole story. Sir Cyril Burt, in spite of his being maligned for saying so, undoubtedly had a point when he maintained that working-class parents produced less bright children than middle-class parents. It seems fairly obvious that if both your parents were doctors, lawyers, engineers or physicists, or some other profession requiring considerable brain power, your chances of inheriting that intellectual calibre is much higher than if your parents were class 5 or unskilled labourers. It doesn't always follow, but it is more probable. It is the old 'nature versus nurture' argument, but nature usually comes out on top.

It is very fashionable nowadays to talk about developing 'language skills' and to maintain that reading skills should not be attempted until language has made for reading readiness. However, any teacher, remedial or otherwise, will bring the development of language into the reading process by linking it to writing and the proper grammatical construction of sentences.

Since it is now generally understood that dyslexia is a language disorder, it may be helpful to look at language disorders as a whole to realize that there is considerable overlap.

Eighty per cent of children with delayed or disordered speech and/or language development have later problems with written language – probably accounting for their lack of phonological awareness. This can best be understood by referring to the Venn diagram in Figure 4.1, which clearly indicates the overlap between the various language disabilities, ranging from very mild to very severe.

As you will see, dyslexia in its mildest form affects only written language and spelling, but as the condition deepens, reading is also involved and many aphasic symptoms creep in, such as inability to tell the time, problems

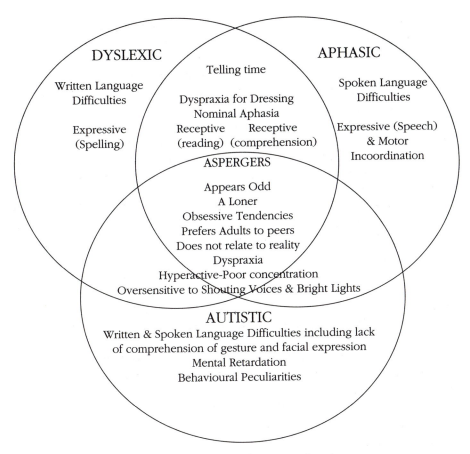

Figure 4.1: Venn diagram showing overlap of language disorders.
© Bevé Hornsby 1994.

with the concept of time, lack of co-ordination for fine or gross motor movement (dyspraxia or clumsiness), word-finding difficulties, problems with left and right, and general disorganization. The severe dyslexic may have many of the autistic characteristics, such as preferring adults to peers, tending to be a loner, obsessive tendencies, difficulty differentiating between fact and fiction, poor concentration and oversensitivity to shouting voices and bright lights. This condition is usually referred to as Asperger's syndrome, after the paediatrician who first diagnosed it.

The autistic child is, of course, in deep trouble since, although he can see and hear, he cannot make sense of what he sees and hears, not even gestures or facial expressions, and everything has to be taught. Fortunately, the condition is rare and, as with dyslexia, it affects many more boys than girls.

The Americans, who were the first to take 'developmental dyslexia' seriously, through Samuel T Orton's work in the 1930s, describe dyslexia quite clearly as a language disorder, since language, be it spoken or written, is still language. The system that was subsequently devised under Orton's guidance at the Scottish Rite Hospital in Texas by Bessie Stillman (a teacher) and Anna Gillingham (a psychologist) was known as 'A language course for teachers and pupils'. An adapted version of this programme is now available in the UK, written by Auger and Briggs (1992). Strangely enough, although the programme contained very little teaching of language as we understand it, it was very thorough on the scientific approach to spelling, and through spelling, to reading.

The Orton–Gillingham teaching programme has had a profound effect on all the 'multisensory programmes' that have been produced since (including *Alpha to Omega*) and has proved both effective and durable. If training colleges and government would understand the tenets contained in these programmes, our literacy problem would have an opportunity to be solved. The present Minister for Education, the Rt Hon David Blunkett, certainly has some very good and sensible ideas, but they need to be spelled out in detail if teachers are to be able to understand and to implement them.

As Lord Melbourne said in the 1830s, when he was prime minister, 'All are agreed about the benefits of education, but are unable to agree as to the means of carrying them into effect'.

Not much has changed in the last 171 years!

References

Auger J, Briggs S (1992) *The Hickey Multi-sensory Language Course*. London: Whurr Publishers.

Lenneberg EH (1967) *The Biological Foundations of Language*. New York: John Wiley.

Orton ST (1930) *Incidence of Language Disorder Leading to Dyslexia*. Cambridge MA. Educators Publishing Service Inc.

Stillman A, Gillingham B (1969) *Remedial Training for Children with Specific Disability in Reading, Spelling and Penmanship*. Cambridge MA: Educators Publishing Service Inc.

CHAPTER 5

Current trends in language disability

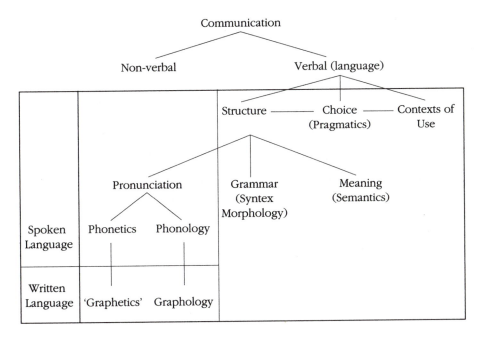

Figure 5.1: Current trends in language disability: a linguistic perspective.

The main dimensions of language study

- Syntax: the study of sentence structure.
- Morphology: the structure of a word and how it can be extended, e.g. nation, national, nationalization.
- Pragmatics: practical usage.
- Phonetics: sounds.
- Graphetics: letters.

Before it is possible to diagnose a language disorder or delay it is necessary to be fully conversant with normal development. The full developmental milestones can be obtained from the *Stycar Chart of Developmental Sequences* (Sheridan 1971), but a simplified guide to speech and language development is as follows.

- First words with meaning, 1 year.
- Word order in phrases, 2 years: Daddy kick.
- Extended phrases, 2½ years: Daddy kick ball; Daddy kick big ball.
- Full sentences, 3 years: My Daddy kick big ball.
- Indefinite extension by use of the word 'and' by 3½ years.

Thus grammar at first level is phrase structure, at second level clause structure and at third level sentence structure.

There is often a period of non-fluency around 3½ to 4 years, which does not usually progress to stammering unless some emotional stress is introduced at that time.

By 3½ grammar is not usually perfect, e.g. 'me hate mouses'. By 4½ grammar should be correct and by 5 language acquisition should be complete (Sheridan 1971). All that will be acquired after that is a more sophisticated vocabulary. Syntax comes before morphology and there are parallels between speaking and writing.

Graphology is the writing system of a language and how it is set out, and since handwriting is a learned motor skill it needs to be correctly taught from the beginning.

David Crystal believes that success in reading and writing depends on listening and speaking skills – in other words, literacy depends on oracy.

The question then needs to be asked: are dyslexics always deficient in earlier speaking skills in either production or comprehension? Crystal believes they are, but detection is often difficult as the deficiencies tend to be subtle and difficult to detect, particularly with regard to comprehension.

Order of mention syndrome

People with comprehension difficulties tend to do the thing that is mentioned first without waiting for the full command to be understood. The most difficult sequences to appreciate are:

- Do X THEN Y.
- Do X BEFORE Y.
- Do X AFTER Y.

For example if the teacher says: 'Before you go out to play do ...', they hear 'go out to play' first, so they do it first without waiting for the do ....

There is also a graphology/phonology relationship and basically there are only two things that can go wrong in spoken or written language, except in a totally language-disordered child where everything has gone wrong!

It is essential to be able to pinpoint what these are in Figure 5.1, in order to instigate appropriate remediation, but they relate to either production or comprehension.

From diagram to intervention

Look first at normal language development and note any disparities. The verb is the word to look out for as language-delayed/disordered children do not use action words. Trying to help them understand with verb picture cards is not always helpful because the card is static whereas the verb denotes action. Noun cards are easy – what is this or that. But 'What is the man doing?' requires a verb in the answer and they haven't got any.

So, what about imitation?

• The man is sleeping – the man is ...?

Or choice.

• 'Is he eating or drinking?'

Of course, early intervention, which requires early and accurate diagnosis, is the key. As the child gets older intervention becomes more and more difficult because so many different and often conflicting things have been taught, which are almost impossible to unravel. So the message is: *catch him before he is five*, as birth to five is the critical period for acquiring spoken language.

References

Crystal D (1987) *Concept of language development: a realistic perspective*. In *Language Development and Language Disorders* (eds W Yule, M Rutter). Oxford: Mackeith Press.

Sheridan M (1971) *The Stycar Chart of Developmental Sequences*. Windsor: NFER Nelson Publishing Co.

Further reading

Rinaldi WF (2000) Pragmatic comprehension in secondary-aged students with specific developmental language disorders. *International Journal of Language and Communication Disorders* **35**(1).

Vance M, Wells W (1994) The wrong end of the stick: language impaired children's comprehension of non-literal language. *Child Language, Teaching & Therapy* **10**: 23–46.

Yule W, Rutter M (eds) *Language Development and Language Disorders*. Oxford: Mackeith Press.

CHAPTER 6

Careers for dyslexics

Dyslexics and the job market

I am not too happy about the concept of looking at careers specifically for dyslexics, as this suggests that they are a subgroup within the general population who are likely to be handicapped in respect of the careers they may wish, or are likely to be able, to follow.

I wish to stress from the outset that this is not necessarily the case. As long as the dyslexia has been recognized and suitable treatment provided, there is no reason why the individual's initial handicap should not have been sufficiently overcome for him or her to pursue whatever profession or trade that happens to be of interest.

Choice of career

As with everybody, choice of career depends on a number of factors.

- Where the professions are concerned, children often follow similar paths to their parents, since they have been brought up in an atmosphere which is likely to generate knowledge and interest in that profession. The same is probably true of other occupations.
- The intellectual level of the person in question. Professions such as medicine, the law, academic professors, top-level scientists and engineers, architects and so on do require a considerable amount of high-calibre grey matter to be able to cope with the amount of information that has to be ingested in order to successfully follow careers of this nature.
- The interests and aptitudes of the individuals concerned need to be taken into account so that they are not pushed or squeezed into occupations that are abhorrent to them.
- Given that due consideration had been given to the above, it is essential that realistic goals are set, not only for the person seeking employment but also with regard to the job market both now and in the future.

Attention also needs to be given to the type of jobs that are likely to be in demand by employers.

Spatial ability

There is a gut feeling among clinicians and researchers in the field of dyslexia that dyslexics are likely to have exceptional spatial ability and tend to succeed in occupations requiring such skills. There has been very little systematic research into this aspect and so far no firm evidence to support the view that spatial ability is more prevalent among dyslexics than in the general population. Such evidence should be forthcoming shortly, when a Department for Education and Science-sponsored follow-up of a substantial number of proven dyslexics has been published and one or two other follow-ups completed.

Dr Margaret Rawson, in her book *Developmental Language Disability* published in the USA in 1968, did include a survey on the occupations of 56 dyslexic boys and their fathers, the results of which are shown in Table 6.1.

However, in Margaret Rawson's table of occupations, the highest number of boys following spatially orientated jobs is not apparent. Research scientists, college professors, middle management, lawyers, medium management and own businesses are the most popular, in that order.

Dr MacFarlane Smith, in his book *Spatial Ability*, presents an enormous list of occupations considered to require top-level spatial ability as prepared by the US Employment Service. A shortened version puts such categories as draughtsmen, engineers and surgeons under one heading rather than specifying all the possible variations in opportunities within those headings.

Businessman is not included in MacFarlane Smith's list, nor is salesman or caterer/chef, although a large number of dyslexics have succeeded in these fields. However, a number of dyslexics show an aptitude for art, music, drama, literature and even languages, and should not be discouraged from following this bent in spite of the possibility of difficulties in passing the requisite examinations. Most art colleges and music colleges will waive some of these requirements, in any case, if a student shows outstanding gifts.

Among fathers, lawyers and professional engineers top the previous lists. A similar distribution was found in this survey. In the UK, it is particularly noticeable that many dyslexics are verbally articulate – have the 'gift of the gab' – and hence politicians figure widely in this group as do lecturers, lawyers, actors and actresses. On the other hand, those who started life with a severe language disability do seem to have continuing problems, like the young man whose language impairment made it impossible for me to administer the verbal scale on the WISC, while obtaining a performance IQ of 125. He eventually obtained an NVQ in horticulture and was employed by the London Parks Department, but only on a temporary basis as he invariably failed the interviews for a permanent position because of his inability to express himself adequately.

Table 6.1: Occupations – 56 boys and their parents

Occupations	Boys	Fathers	Mothers
Doctor	2	2	0
Lawyer	4	10	0
Clergyman	0	1	0
College administrator	0	3	0
College professor	6	9	1
College instructor	1	1	0
Research scientist	8	1	0
Economist, research, consultation or arbitration	0	4	0
Professional engineer	1	9	0
Artist, designer	0	1	0
Actor (supporting, on contract)	1	0	0
Architect	0	1	0
City planner	1	0	0
Community organization (director)	1	0	2
Social worker (in-service trained)	1	0	1
School principal	1	0	0
School teacher, MA	1	1	9
School teacher, BA	2	0	9
School teacher, no degree	1	0	8
Business, owner or manager			
Large	0	4	0
Medium	4	1	0
'Middle management' (junior executive)	7	2	0
Business, minor official	2	4	1
Sales representative, technical	3	1	0
Management trainee	1	0	0
Skilled labourer, or foreman	2	1	0
Semi-skilled labourer, or apprentice	2	0	0
Housewife	0	0	25
Two or more occupations (e.g. minor business job and own medium-size business)	4	0	0
Unemployed	0	0	0
Total	56	56	56

Source: Rawson (1968)

Table 6.2: The most common occupations among the fathers of dyslexics I have known

- Actor
- Advertising
- Agriculture/farming
- Ambulance service
- Antique dealer
- Architect
- Armed services
- Artist
- Barrister
- Bricklayer
- Builder
- Cameraman
- Car mechanic
- Carpenter
- Caterer
- Clothing business
- Computer programmer/operator/consultant
- Company director of own company
- Construction work
- Cook/chef
- Craftsman
- Dancer
- Decorator
- Dentist
- Designer (graphic, fashion, industrial, interior, stage)
- Doctor
- Draughtsman
- Dressmaking
- Driver (bus, train, truck)
- Electrician
- Engineer
- Entrepreneur
- Factory worker
- Fire service
- Forestry
- Gardener (landscape, market, nurseryman)
- General practitioner
- Hairdresser
- Insurance underwriter
- Lawyer
- Lecturer
- Mechanic
- Merchant navy
- Motor mechanic
- Musician
- Nurse
- Optician
- Osteopath
- Painter
- Petroleum exploration
- Photographer
- Physiotherapist
- Pilot
- Plumber
- Police
- Politician
- Printing
- Reprographics
- Salesman
- Scientist
- Shop assistant
- Solicitor
- Sports
- Surgeon
- Surveying
- Veterinary surgeon
- Welding

References

Macfarlane Smith I (1964) *Spatial Ability*. London: London University Press.

Rawson MB (1968). *Developmental Language Disability: adult accomplishments of dyslexic boys*. Baltimore: Johns Hopkins Press.

CHAPTER 7

Literacy and careers

Examinations

Unfortunately, examinations now play a much greater part in the UK than they did in, say, the 1960s. At that time nearly half the school population started work without any formal qualifications. Now, seven out of eight school-leavers have at least one Certificate of Secondary Education. In other words, exam passes have become a kind of currency which children and their parents expect to be able to trade in for a better job. It is not necessarily so, of course. In fact, a degree can often be a passport to unemployment as few firms like taking on someone who is over-qualified for the job that is on offer.

Too many young people now have degrees, often in virtually useless subjects. Nevertheless, it gives them illusions of grandeur and dissatisfaction with 'life' if the doors of opportunity do not open for them immediately. This imbalance is currently being modified in that university grants are being cut back so that fewer students can be accepted and only the really able ones are likely to succeed in obtaining places – which is as it should be. Similarly, the baby boom of the 1950s has been replaced by the baby bust of the 1960s, 1970s and 1980s, which means that fewer young people of 18 to 24 are entering the workforce now.

Careers requiring examinations

Certain careers do require examination qualifications to ensure that prospective candidates have sufficient brain power to cope with the workload that is going to be expected of them. That is only the beginning of the story, of course, as final selection usually hinges on an interview to ensure that the person in question has the right sort of personality, appearance and aptitude for the proposed career they wish to follow. Fewer places does mean more stringent selection, which should lead to more suitable

31

candidates being selected – small is, indeed, becoming beautiful in more ways than one, as Schumacher predicted.

Until recently, the high-IQ occupations were also the well-paid occupations. The correlation between fathers' and sons' income is at least 0.4 if not 0.5. However, over the past decade another class of high earner has arisen, namely the chairmen or chief executives of big corporate businesses, such as Richard Branson or Arthur McAlpine, both of whom I believe are, or were, dyslexic. They must certainly have had their fair share of quality brain cells if earning power comes into the equation.

However, none of these facts should deter the dyslexic who has received the right help and has the natural ability and motivation to enter the fray and succeed.

Adult dyslexics

For those for whom the train has already left the station and who are on their way into the journey of life without the benefit of current knowledge, understanding or suitable specialist help, the picture is somewhat different. Most adults have sorted the situation out for themselves and developed their own strategies for coping with semi-literacy in a literate world, or they have taken an unconventional road, which may well be antisocial.

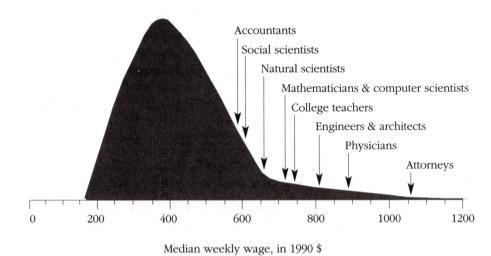

Median weekly wage, in 1990 $

Figure 7.1: The recent American wage distribution

Source: US Department of Labor (1991)

In many ways, reading is not as significant as it was because television and radio provide a wealth of information which can be gleaned without the ability to read. Public signs have mainly been replaced by drawings. Not, of course, to help the non-reader, but as an international agreement to help travellers; things such as 'Gents' and 'Ladies', which might have caused confusion and embarrassment 10 years ago, now have more easily recognizable signs, although one still comes across 'Toilets'.

Figure 7.2: Non-linguistic signs.

Public signs may be observed everywhere in the environment, and you still see: 'In', 'Out', 'Entrance', 'Exit', 'Push', 'Pull', 'Saloon Bar', 'Restaurant', 'Parking', 'Public', 'Private', 'Pay Here', 'Slow', 'Police', 'Caution', 'Danger', 'Doctor', 'First Aid', 'Keep Off The Grass' and so on.

When travelling by train, people who cannot read may find it difficult to recognize the station they wish to get out at, and may need to ask someone for help, either the ticket collector or another passenger.

Reading maps can be a nightmare, especially if there is directional confusion as well. Following landmarks is fairly easy, but having a navigator is better.

Passing the driving test does not seem to present too many problems as the Highway Code can be learnt by heart by having someone put it on tape and the road signs are self-explanatory. Unfortunately, a written exam has recently been introduced, but it consists of multiple choice questions only, which are not too daunting.

Filling in forms usually requires the dyslexic adult to admit that he or she does not understand them and ask for an official to do it for them. There is no shame in this, as few people really understand official forms!

Being able to write a cheque is essential if you wish to have a bank account and understanding your bank statement is useful too! I have seldom met anyone who did not understand when they were overdrawn, however.

The biggest problem that I have encountered in the severely handicapped adult seems to be their fear of being expected to take down telephone messages. There are two ways round this. You can either have a sophisticated link-up with a tape recorder on to which the message can be transmitted or you can legitimately ask the person to spell their name carefully and slowly and also their address and telephone number.

Everybody should do this automatically in any case if they wish to take down messages correctly. The person who doesn't is a menace.

The telephone, or indeed a tape recorder or electronically produced voice as in the game 'Speak and Spell' handles only a limited frequency range so that certain sounds are easily confused or distorted. For example, /b/ often sounds like /v/ and vice versa; /f/, /s/ and /th/ are often indistinguishable. This is why, when messages are being transmitted by means of radio or telephone a code is used for identifying sounds, such as:

- C for Charlie
- F for Freddie
- E for egg
- B for brother
- S for sugar
- V for Vera.

It is a pity that many of them are linked to the spelling rather than the sound, so the dyslexic will need his or her own code to impose on the person giving the message when checking it back for correctness.

Fortunately, most severely dyslexic adults discover that the best answer is a literate partner or secretary, or preferably both, who will do the reading and writing and leave him or her to get on with having the ideas and doing the job.

Happily, there are few adults who are so severely handicapped. Most learn to read sufficiently well to get by, even if writing still presents problems. And there is always the telephone for communication purposes, or even a 'talking notebook' on to which letters can be dictated for later transcription. In any case there is no shame attached to dyslexia, and learning to live with the problem, as one has to learn to live with most problems, is the best answer.

The college student

People tend to assume that once a student has made it to college he or she will not need any further help. This may be true, but there are those who find a degree course an enormous strain. Taking comprehensible notes from a lecture is often impossible. However, there are four possible solutions.

- If you have a very good memory, just listen hard, make only minimal jottings to jog your memory and then write up as much as you can retain in the evening, double-checking with a friend to see if you have missed anything vital. This will not usually be a burden, and he or she may be glad to discuss the subject to fill in any points they missed.

- Take a tape recorder to lectures and record them. You may have to ask the lecturer if he or she minds, but usually they do not. However, this is time-consuming, as you will then have to listen to the tape several times in your spare time and make notes of the salient points.
- Ask a friend to make a copy of his or her notes using carbon paper. Again, you can discuss the notes and the lecture later, which will benefit both of you.
- Have a laptop computer. However, you will need fast keyboard skills to use this effectively.

Another useful skill is to learn how to abstract information from textbooks without having to read the book from cover to cover.

- Read the contents page.
- Decide which chapters are likely to be useful.
- Then read the summary at the end of the chapter.
- Discover how to use the index to find specific facts within the text.
- Transfer the important points contained in the book to an index file in alphabetical order by author surname, giving the full reference of the book thus: Goodman VF (1975) *The Life Cycle of the Centipede.* London: Longmans.

Fill as many cards as necessary with the facts contained in the book, numbering them as you go. Keep a separate index file for each subject you are studying. In this way you will reduce the amount of essential material that will need to be revised before an exam and will have the full references immediately to hand when writing essays. These should be annotated at the end of the essay as follows.

- Names of books are underlined or italicized and the main words of the title all begin with capital letters, e.g. *The History of the World.*
- Journal articles are not underlined and do not use capitals except for the first word. The title of the journal is underlined or italicized and the volume number is emboldened, e.g. A study of the reaction of a fly to a spider's web. *Journal of Biological Research* **6**: 126–131.

Of course, the author's name and date of publication precede the above, as discussed before. All references should be arranged in alphabetical order according to the author's surname.

Handwriting

If your handwriting is poor or indeed, even if it is not, a typewritten essay in one and a half or double-line spacing with good margins is much more acceptable and professional-looking than handwritten work. A great deal of weight is often given on a continuous assessment basis to essay work done throughout the course. If you can manage As or Bs your chances of obtaining a good degree are increased. Learning how to type will stand you in good stead throughout your life.

Examination techniques

Do not rush to begin writing the moment you are given the word to turn over the examination paper. Read it slowly and carefully, making sure you have understood what is required. Make doubly sure which questions are compulsory and which are voluntary, and how many questions you must answer in all. Decide which ones you are going to choose from the non-obligatory questions and then start writing. By this time your hands will have probably stopped shaking so that you can write.

I do not advocate making notes first as this takes up too much of the precious 25 minutes or so which you can spend on each answer, but as the theme develops while you write, other important points will occur to you. Jot those down *immediately*, otherwise when you reach the appropriate point to bring them in you will have forgotten what they were!

Try to give yourself 10 minutes at the end to check your answers if you possibly can. On the other hand, if you are still writing furiously when the examination comes to a close, do not bother – you have probably done pretty well in any case.

Do make a list of the specialized vocabulary needed for each subject and ensure that you can spell all the words correctly. Learn at least one new sophisticated word each week and use it appropriately in your essays so that it becomes familiar enough to use it in the exams. If you build up a good vocabulary of apt and learned words it raises the quality of your writing at once. Choose words that are not too difficult to spell but that are commonly misused by the general public. It will be a feather in your cap if you use them correctly. Take militate and mitigate for example – very easy to spell but very commonly misused:

* militate: from the word militant, fighting: engaged in warfare. To serve as a soldier; to contend. 'Militate against' means to fight for a cause, to give weight to an argument; tell against

- mitigate: means to mollify or appease; to make more easily borne; to lessen the severity. Mitigating circumstances: circumstances which lessen the severity of the crime.

Familiarize yourself with connectives to make your written language flow. 'Not only' should be followed by 'but also'. For example: 'Not only was the army in disarray, but also exhausted and dispirited.'

Use descriptive words as much as possible. 'A dark night' can also be 'A dark, wet, stormy night, with the wind whistling through the cracks of the ill-fitting doors and windows like icy tentacles which clutched at our already half-frozen hands and feet and nipped the ends of our blue noses.' Not a single difficult word in that passage but it does give some idea of atmosphere!

Use 'nevertheless', 'however', 'therefore', 'indeed', 'because', 'in the face of', 'fortunately', 'unhappily' and so on to connect your thoughts. For example: 'It was, however, a bad idea to come across country as the distance we saved was counteracted by the energy we had to expend in dragging our weary feet through the thick mud!'

Look up the word 'count' and 'counter' – they occupy a page and a half in a standard dictionary. You will be surprised to find how many meanings and usages they have.

Make your dictionary a friend; it will not only provide you with the meaning of words, but also tell you how to pronounce them and how to use them in sentences. To do this to greatest advantage you will need to jot down each word you do not know the meaning of and look them up later. In this way you will build up your written vocabulary and improve your style. Keep a personal dictionary so you can be constantly referring to it and familiarizing yourself with your new words. Much poor English can be attributed to sheer poverty of vocabulary as well as poor sentence structure. When reading, make a note of how famous authors use words and sentence construction to get their meaning across.

Avoid ambiguity in your sentences. In other words, make sure the reader will know what you intended and whether what you have written makes this clear. For example:

- 'Every year the firemen attend hundreds of fires and every year thousands of people die as a result' would be better phrased as 'Thousands of people die every year as a result of fires, in spite of the fact that firemen are involved in putting out hundreds of fires and rescuing thousands of people'.

- 'The chairman remarked that in the circumstances the society could not employ a better secretary' would be better phrased as 'The chairman remarked that the company could not have a better secretary, whatever the circumstances'.

Finally, you learn English by using it. Using language by reading, writing, listening and talking is the best and only way to acquire the skills of communication.

Recommended reading

Hornsby B (1997) *Overcoming Dyslexia: a straightforward guide for families and teachers*, 3rd edn. London: Random House UK.

CHAPTER 8

Teaching methods

We have read in this book and elsewhere what dyslexia is, and how the dyslexic differs from the normal reader, or even from the reader challenged in other ways. I would now like to go into the question of teaching – I hate that word 'remediation'. As with the identification of the condition, the method of treating it emanated from the medical profession rather than from education. It was from the seeds sown in the 1930s by neurologist Samuel Orton (1937), that Bessie Stillman and Anna Gillingham developed their teaching method (Stillman & Gillingham 1969). And the methods now used in all the centres where the concept of dyslexia is taken seriously have drawn their inspiration and structure from the work of Edith Norrie, a speech therapist in Denmark. (The Edith Norrie Letter Case is now published by The Helen Arkell Dyslexia Centre, Frensham, Farnham, Surrey GU10 3BW.) The Americans call their method multisensory, but I prefer to call it circular.

One must bear in mind the symbolic nature of language and the sensory/motor nature of the central nervous system when devising any teaching method that involves language development and neurological deficits, no matter how 'soft' these neurological deficits may be.

If one is feeding information into the system from all the senses (auditory, visual and tactile), processing this information, translating it into motor activities (in either speech or writing) and then feeding it back in again via the kinesthetic feedback system, it matters not where the breakdown in the circuit has occurred, since the circularity of the teaching will eventually bridge the gap.

Methods that are known to be successful, in the majority of cases, are based on a phonetic, structured, sequential, cumulative and thorough approach to the teaching of total language skills – not just reading, but spelling, writing and expressing oneself coherently on paper.

I am tempted to quote an eminent psychiatrist who said that 'where the mind is concerned we are not in the Middle Ages, we are in the Dark Ages!

If you find something that works, for God's sake latch on to it, and don't ask too many damn fool questions!'. His words, not mine!

He was, as it happens referring to the therapeutic effect of horse riding for the mentally disabled and stressed that the better bred the horse, the more effective was the rapport – just any old sluggard of a horse wouldn't do. And the same thing applies to teaching – the higher the quality of the teacher the better the rapport and chances of success.

Again referring to riding, it was said that these children were ordinary children with a mental disability just as others may be ordinary children with an optical disability, an auditory disability or a dyslexic disability.

One is not seeking to 'cure' that disability (although this can happen) but to help them to reach the ceiling of their capabilities. What one is doing is rather like pushing a pipe cleaner up the blocked conduits of the mind so that the pathway to understanding what reading and spelling is all about is gradually, or in some cases suddenly, revealed. I am constantly being told that there are dozens of ways of teaching people to read, and what we are doing is old fashioned and narrow.

Tom Crabtree will tell you that all you have to do is find a book that interests the dyslexic, whether it's on 'torture', 'guns', 'contraceptives' or 'golf'; but sadly it is not that simple. If that was all that was needed, he or she would have learnt to read long ago. The subject matter may be of interest; but the skills to decipher it are lacking.

It is rather like saying that in some countries they drive on the left-hand side of the road and some on the right, and both methods work. In Istanbul, they drive in the middle of the road and it is said that there are no bad drivers in Turkey because they are all dead. It is a pity that educational mismanagement is lethal only to the child.

'Look and Say' and the Initial Teaching Alphabet (ITA) have both proved to be a disaster for the dyslexic; but brilliant teachers can take the middle road between sight word teaching and phonetics, and meld them together to produce a coherent whole.

At Bart's, where it all started, being a hospital clinic the caseload was wide and varied, ranging in age from 5½ to 46, and we treated acquired dyslexia as well as developmental dyslexia, and some people with multiple disabilities.

There seems little doubt then that, like Heineken beer, we seemed able to refresh the parts that other teaching could not reach. As Bonnie Macmillan (1997) so rightly says:

> What is required now that we have proved what works is to introduce this knowledge into the Teacher Training Colleges so that every teacher will have completed a module on the teaching of children with Specific Learning Difficulties/dyslexia and the children will reap the benefit.

Our thanks though should go to the children who have suffered so much and taught us so much. It is both a privilege and a pain to be working with them. If you care for children the time is *now* – the means are here; there need be no delay.

Most writers on the teaching of reading assume that all children have made a start on the road to literacy and talk glibly about miscue analysis, reading for meaning, a psycholinguistic guessing game and end up by advocating an eclectic approach incorporating 'phonics' and sight words.

Indeed, you can do that, but only if the principles behind both methods are fully understood. In the Warnock Report (1978) it was stated that 20% of children were likely to have difficulties in acquiring the basic skills of reading, writing, spelling and numeracy at some point in their school careers. Surely it makes sense, therefore, to teach to the 20% who are likely to have difficulties and allow the 80% who will learn by whatever method happens to be in fashion at the time to go ahead, but with an enhanced knowledge of English, its grammar, syntax and usage. Only in this way can we solve the near disastrous state to which our literacy standards have fallen in the past 15 years.

Dr Bernard Lamb, in his 1997 survey of teachers of English, found that up to 85% of leavers from comprehensives and colleges of further education were very poor at written English, *in the opinion of their teachers*, yet the majority of teachers of English (two out of three) were *against* the explicit systematic teaching of spelling and grammar. Perhaps because their own knowledge is deficient? One teacher made seven errors in 15 lines. These included plural subjects with singular verbs, wrong commas and apostrophes, and spellings such as grammer, burocratic and goverment.

Employers have a similar view, and in an earlier survey, Dr Lamb (1997) found that 94% of employers said that the schools were doing an inadequate job of teaching English and communication skills.

The term phoneme/grapheme relationship is unclear in teachers' minds because neither is ever explained in articles on the teaching of reading and spelling. A phoneme is the smallest unit of sound that will change the meaning of a word. Thus: chat contains three phonemes and string contains five, the 'g' being understood because of the velarization of the 'n'. A grapheme is a class of letter/letters etc. representing a phoneme. Therefore, these letters need to be given names to make it possible to describe all the different combinations of letters required to produce the 24 consonant sounds and 20 vowel sounds that comprise the English language, in other words, 26 letters in 300 combinations.

No teacher can possibly understand and explain to children the spelling patterns of English unless he or she has studied phonetics, which is the science of speech sounds: how they are made in isolation; how they are affected by the context in which they appear in words; and how they are distorted in running speech.

It is as different from what is commonly understood by 'phonics' as a child playing a five-finger exercise on the piano is from a concert pianist playing a Beethoven sonata. Most people, including teachers, interpret the teaching of reading and spelling as simply teaching children the 26 sounds of the letters of the alphabet instead of their names. This philosophy is flawed, because names are easier than sounds, appear developmentally at an earlier age and most children start school already knowing the names. They are then not allowed to use them, although they learn the alphabet song, which is rendered meaningless when it is not used in the context of reading and spelling.

Sadly, Montessori teaching, which is so good in so many ways, only teaches sounds and lower-case letters – again putting the cart before the horse since capitals are so much easier to learn than lower-case letters and can be copied by a child of three whose pencil control enables him or her to copy a circle and a straight line. Similarly, letterland makes the same mistake by using fantacized alphabet names rather than the correct ones and teaches only the 26 sounds. It is remarkable that the majority (80%) manage to learn in spite of this flawed technique, but 20% cannot and this is where the commonsense of dyslexia-orientated teaching comes to the rescue.

When Rab Butler masterminded the educational reform in 1944, making secondary education compulsory for all, he envisaged three grades of school:

- gold: grammar school
- silver: technical college
- copper: secondary modern.

The 11+ was introduced and IQ ruled the schools' lives. Every school was required to start with religious assembly and religious education was compulsory. It was thought that state schools would become so good that private schools would wither away. This belief was sadly unfounded and private schools have flourished and proliferated. Even private schools do not always understand how to help dyslexics, but they are improving.

The trouble is that dyslexia falls between two stools – medicine and education. Hospitals do not really want to be involved and teachers are not trained to handle it. So what to do? Education has merely changed the name to specific learning difficulties (SLDs) to avoid the term dyslexia. However, that does not solve the problem, it only adds to the confusion.

As Frank Muir said in a dissertation on semantics: 'Sight and vision may be considered to mean the same thing, but if you call a woman a vision, it is quite different to calling her a sight!'

Thus dyslexia is easily understood, but SLDs can often be mistaken for general learning difficulties – in other words, below average intelligence. As Dr WS Parker, the MOH for Brighton so rightly said: 'Teachers take refuge in the magic inaccuracy of Specific Reading Disability.' Dyslexia comes on the fringe of the experience of many professions, but in the middle of the field of interest to none.

References

Butler RA (1944) *The Education Act.* London: The Stationery Office.

Lamb BC (1997) Teachers' views on English standards, grammar teaching, the correction of errors, and on each other. In *Controversial Issues in English 1997.* The Proceedings of the Silver Jubilee Conference of the Queen's English Society. London: The Queen's English Society.

Macmillan B (1997) *Why School Children Can't Read.* London: Institute of Economic Affairs.

Orton ST (1937) *Reading, Writing and Speech Problems in Children.* London: Chapman & Hall.

Stillman A, Gillingham B (1969) *Remedial Training for Children with Specific Disability in Reading, Spelling and Penmanship.* Cambridge MA: Educators Publishing Service Inc.

Warnock M (1978) *The Warnock Report.* London: The Stationery Office.

CHAPTER 9

Reach for the stars with *Alpha to Omega*: a detailed description of a multisensory programme

Figure 9.1: The west window of St Nicholas Church, Moreton, Dorset. A Spin of Galaxy, engraved by Lawrence Whistler. Discovered by Tina and Micheal Jubb.

Alpha to Omega, the A–Z of Teaching Reading, Writing and Spelling (Hornsby et al. 1999) is not only the most widely used multisensory programme in the field of SLDs/dyslexia, but is also the most comprehensive, taking children through all the requirements of the National Curriculum for English from Stage 1 through to Stage 6.

Alpha to Omega was the first of the phonetic, linguistic, structured, sequential programmes to be published in the UK, as well as the first to be written by a speech therapist. Hence, the phonetic knowledge that is brought to bear on the teaching of English is considerable and far exceeds that normally acquired by qualified teachers. Perhaps this is why it has proved so successful in mitigating a multitude of learning difficulties, which takes it outside the somewhat narrow range of dyslexia. Indeed, at Hornsby House, it is used as standard practice throughout the nursery and reception classes as well as higher up the school if required.

Quite simply, multisensory means using all the senses of hearing, saying, doing and kinesthetic feedback from the muscles to the brain to tell the individual what it is that he or she has done. However, that is not all that is required as it is the step-by-step approach that makes the learning clearly understood. And, as the children are never asked to do anything they have not been specifically taught or happen to know, errorless learning takes place and a sense of success and achievement is born, which is what generates confidence.

Step one, as Sir Ron Dearing, Chairman of the Schools Curriculum Assessment Authority, rightly points out, is that all children need to know the tools of literacy – namely, the letters of the Roman alphabet (Dearing 1997). They need to know the names, the sounds associated with the names, and the shapes, both capitals and lower case, print and handwriting, which must be correctly taught from the beginning of schooling and always on lines.

Step two. As soon as single letter/sound associations have been grasped, the letters need to be synthesized for reading and analysed for spelling, and used meaningfully in sentences so that correct grammar and punctuation can be introduced early on.

Step three. The letters then need to be chunked together to represent all 44 sounds of the English language in the following order:

- consonant digraphs – sh, ch, th (the voiceless sound, as in 'thin'), TH (the voiced sound, as in 'the')
- consonant blends, double and then triple – bl, dr, spr, thr.

They need to know the five basic vowels and the semi-vowel 'y', which has the same vowel sound properties as 'i'. They need to know that every word and every syllable must contain at least one vowel.

Step four is the realization that some vowels have a long sound, which is the same as the letter's name and that this occurs when the syllable is open – that is, ending in a vowel such as 'be', 'my', 'go'. There are drills in *Alpha to Omega* for teaching reading, spelling and writing, which need to be strictly adhered to for maximum effect.

In fact, there is an order to everything and the reason for the order is known. For example, capital letters should be taught first because they are developmentally the first form of letter that a child can produce, since most children of three can copy a straight line and a circle. Capital letters are all variations of straight lines and circles and are, therefore, easier to reproduce.

- They are all the same size and have no complications such as ascenders and descenders.
- They all sit on the line.
- The letters do not change when orientation is different, like a cup, which is always understood as a cup, no matter from what angle it is seen.

- Capital letters, like the cup, remain recognizable regardless of which way they are facing:

ꓭ B   ꓷ D   ꟼ P   Q Ɋ

Also, so long as all letters start from the top there are no beginning or ending strokes to complicate matters:

A B C D E F G H I J K L M N O
P Q R S T U V W X Y Z

Of course, all letters and numbers should start from the top, but lower-case letters have different starting points, which need to be inculcated from the beginning as this obviates the problems with b/d, p/q, h/n and m/n, which Rosemary Sassoon calls molehill letters (Sassoon 1990).

There are other reasons for starting with capitals, which prove that they are easier both to learn and to recognize:

- street names are in capitals
- the qwerty keyboard on a typewriter or word processor is in capitals

- car number plates are in capitals
- underground station names are in capitals
- map names are in capitals
- word games are in capitals.

Type 1 – all letters start at the baseline

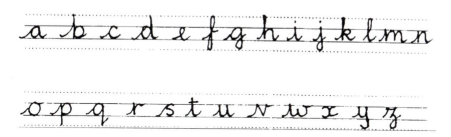

Type 2 – all letters start from their starting point

Another conclusion that we can draw from this is that they are easier and simpler to read and use.

In the same way, names should be taught before sounds, as names are easier and are normally learnt first. They are also important for the understanding of long vowels and to describe letter strings such as digraphs, blends, etc.

Once the child, or adult, is able to synthesize (put together) sounds to make words for reading and to analyse them for spelling, the patterns required for acquiring all the different combinations of letters to both read and spell the 44 sounds gradually unfold in a logical progression. These patterns are then used in structured sentences for both reading and spelling, as suggested in *Alpha to Omega*.

Of course, it will be necessary to acquire a core sight vocabulary of frequently used words, which either do not fit any recognizable pattern or are useful words that can be generalized to help the understanding of less familiar words. For example, if the word 'was' is known, then the spelling rule incorporating the 'magic' qualities of 'w' affecting all vowel sounds that follow it can be easily understood. For example:

> was (the /ă/ has changed to /ŏ/)
>
> thus   want
>   wand
>   wander
>   what
>   wash.

All have an 'a' that sounds like an /ŏ/.

An annotated notebook should be kept of all such words, either already known or taught as sight words throughout the *Alpha to Omega* programme, so that they can always be to hand for ready reference.

One of the best methods for learning odd words is to write the word on a card thus:

$$\boxed{\textbf{said}}$$

Discuss what is unusual about the spelling and the pronunciation. Have the pupil spell the word as many times as necessary, and turn the card over while the pupil spells the word to his or her brain with eyes closed. The pupil then writes the word in his or her exercise book, again spelling it aloud, after which the card is turned face up and the spelling checked. This needs to be done on a regular basis until the word has become internalized.

Of course, real books have their place in any teaching of reading, but should be read to the child or they should be available to listen to on tape until such time as the pupil has sufficient reading competence to read them himself or herself.

There are now a multiplicity of reading schemes that are phonetically graded and would be suitable for a beginning reader, but no child should be expected to read aloud until he or she can do so sufficiently well to avoid embarrassment and loss of self-esteem. All reading should be conducted in the privacy of the one-to-one situation, with suitable help given if necessary, although, to avoid frustration, the reading material provided should always be within the reader's capability.

References

Hornsby B, Shear F, Pool J (1999) *Alpha to Omega – the A–Z of teaching reading, writing and spelling*, 5th edn. Oxford: Heinemann Educational.

Dearing R (1997) *The Dearing Report*. London: The Stationery Office.

Sassoon R (1990) *Handwriting, a New Perspective*. London: Stanley Thornes Publishers.

CHAPTER 10

Readability of print

... a particularly important teaching skill is that of assessing the level of difficulty of books by applying measures of readability. The teacher who can do this is in a better position to match children to reading materials that answer their needs. In our visits to schools we came across many children who were not allowed to read 'real books' until they had completed the scheme. This is an artificial distinction and an unnatural restriction of reading experience. We also came across children who had made good progress through a scheme and were now struggling at frustration level in other kinds of reading, while others were bored by material that was making too few demands on them. The effective teacher is one who has under her conscious control all the resources that can fulfil her purpose. By carefully assessing levels of difficulty she can draw from a variety of sources.

Extract from the Bullock Report. A language for life. London: HMSO (7.32)

John Gilliland (1972) says that readability really means matching reader and text. It has to do with the interest or ease with which a book can be read. Defined by Dale and Chall (1948) as:

The sum of all those elements within a given piece of printed material that affects the success which a group of readers have with it. The success is the extent to which they understand it, read it at optimum speed and find it interesting.

However, there is a good deal more to the total concept of readability than the above might suggest.

The Bullock Report would appear to be relating to the teaching of reading in primary schools, and the undesirability of basing such teaching on 'reading schemes', most of which are designed on word frequency counts and employ a very limited vocabulary with constant repetition as the teaching medium. Children who have learnt to read in this way – that is, by simply memorizing a selected number of words by constant exposure to them – and who have not, in the process, been able to abstract distinctive features of phonetic analysis, letter group probabilities, stress patterns and intonation indicated by punctuation, do have great difficulty when they encounter unfamiliar material. They will not be able to read 'real books', which employ a written vocabulary that is outside their experience, although the words might very well be within their spoken language comprehension. Therefore, the language experience approach to reading may have some value for children whose spoken language is inadequate. These children need to be given the tools for decoding written language, which other children abstract for themselves.

The definition by Dale and Chall (1948) opens up the subject to a greater extent. In the context of 'success that a group of readers have with a text', it takes into account both the reader and the material being read in a broader sense. It not only suggests the actual typography and layout of a book, but also its appearance: whether the cover is inviting or not, whether the book is a convenient size, whether it appeals to the interests of the reader or not and, indeed, on the quality of the paper used, which affects the 'feel' of the book. If one accepts the view that readability is the quality of a written or printed communication that makes it easy for a given class of persons to understand its meaning or that induces them to continue reading, then motivation, personal interests and prior knowledge of the subject are of paramount importance. If one were keen enough, one would presumably struggle through a learned journal article or a manual on motor cycle maintenance regardless of the actual 'readability' of the material. However, if one of the objects of education is to produce a literate society it is essential to consider in considerable detail how best this might be achieved.

Margaret Peters (1971) states that '...the final responsibility is with the teacher who must select, from the material offered, readers that are appropriate to the child's interests, background and idiom. More important still, she must so carefully select the reading level of the book as to give the child not more than a 1 in 20 error rate. For as mistakes increase cues are reduced, interest in the story decreases, and motivation is lost. Indeed, it would be better for the child not to be reading at all than failing to read what is in his hand'.

What then are the factors involved in the ease with which a given passage can be read by a child?

1 Factors in the *reader*: motivation, interest, background and familiarity with the content and vocabulary.
2 Factors in the *print*: type size, leading format and layout.
3 Factors in the *content*: fact, fiction, topic or information.
4 Factors in the *language*: vocabulary, grammar, complexity of structures, style.

5   Factors in the *phonemic structure*: complexities in the phonetic structure of the words used and their logical relationship to sound patterns.

Factors in the reader

Factors in the reader do not lend themselves easily to measurement, since every child will prove to be different in his or her reactions to books. However, it has been noted that the books which have been produced with the environmentally deprived in mind, using the language and situations with which it is presumed the child is familiar, have not proved to be popular in the clinic at Bart's, for example, Leila Berg's *Nippers*. It appears that children do not particularly want to read about the sordid happenings in their everyday lives, but prefer attractive fantasy and mystery and enjoy pictures of clean, nicely dressed children and the sort of parents and homes they might like to have and to live in. Hence the popularity of the Ladybird series in spite of the stilted and almost incomprehensible language of the early readers. Even large print and clear illustrations can hardly help a child to understand a sentence such as 'Look, Peter, look. Have a look. Peter has a look.' What is 'a look'? Who is looking at whom? Is Peter looking or is the reader looking at Peter?

Factors in the print

Factors in the print can certainly be measured. Since speech and language are acquired by the young child through his ability to abstract the distinctive features in a continuous flow of noise around him, and to generalize from this perceptual ability to comprehend more and more complex language forms, so he learns to read by abstracting the distinctive features from the visual 'noise' of print. The more distinguishing features there are, and the more clearly they are presented, must, surely, affect the ability of the child to acquire this visual perceptual skill. It is suggested that the differentiation of easily confused letters (in particular b/d, p/q, g/y, k/h, n/u, m/w) might be assisted by careful variation of the following typography:

- serifs
- heaviness of stroke
- emphasis of distinguishing characteristics
- spacing of letters
- space between words
- width of letters
- interlinear spacing
- margins and general layout.

There are numerous designs of typefaces. Williamson (1966) lists 76, but there are many more now, such as the Rosemary Sassoon (1983, 1991) typefaces, which are becoming popular, although some characteristics are common to many. A short finishing stroke at the top and bottom of a letter is known as a serif. Designs that do not carry these strokes are called sans serif types. Most books are set with serif typeface but sans serif is sometimes used for schoolbooks, particularly readers for young children. The sans serif form is considered more suitable at this stage because it is more like the 'print script' that the pupil is taught to write and the script that tutors tend to use on their flash cards.

Since print, or a serifed typeface, will almost certainly be the choice for a normal reading book it is this that the pupil will have to get used to. Most reading schemes in schools tend to start off with sans serif and progress to serif. Others use Times print throughout, and yet others manuscript throughout.

Some use sans serif and manuscript while introducing the printed 'a' form. There seems to be little consistent policy regarding this, yet it would seem advisable to start with a serifed typeface, since this has been shown to be the most legible (Paterson and Tinker 1940; Walker 1992), and teaching something that later has to be untaught can often prove a stumbling block, particularly to those with poor perception and orientation. The ITA alphabet carried serifs, yet when the changeover to traditional orthography was made, it dropped them, which must have added to the confusion.

It is interesting to note that the Neale Analysis of Reading Ability uses Times print throughout, only the size and boldness becoming less as the passages relate to a higher reading age.

The type size certainly has a considerable effect on readability. Sue Walker of Reading University carried out a pilot study on this facet for the BBC Adult Literacy project. The following type was considered by the students to be the most easily read:

each room it was the same. The
chairs, the tables, the shelves, the
books, were all thick with dust. No
one had been here for a very long time

Other factors were also considered to be of importance.

Interlinear spacing

Interlinear spacing should be such that the lines do not look too close together.

It was a large, gloomy house. There was a   Students found these
tower, like a small church steeple at one   lines too close
end, but apart from this it was not special in   together
any way. It was just the sort of old house

out of the last room. David went over to   Lines set a
the main staircase. But he stopped. For   comfortable
Pam had stopped. He looked back to   distance
her, and she was standing in the doorway   apart

Word spacing

Contrary to good typographic practice for fluent readers, a fairly wide space should be used to give clear separation of words, and a double word space at the end of each sentence. This is of particular value to the disabled reader who has such difficulty in appreciating punctuation and, therefore, the completion of a sentence or sense unit.

But he stopped. For Pam had
stopped. He looked back to her, and
she was standing in the doorway

It will also be noted from the serifed and sans serifed examples given that the serif type is more acceptable and provides more distinguishing features.

At the clinic at Bart's we believed this to be the case and our flash cards are produced in Times print. This is because the pupil is using the reading process when he translates this letter into sound. He is then required to write the letter in 'handwriting', saying the name of the letter as he does so, thus translating sound into its written form. He then reads what he has written by repeating the sound, the rationale being that an association is taught from the beginning between printed and written forms of letters and that both can be read and used for written communication. Thus:

A a *a a* **a** a   are all the family of 'a'

G g *g g* **G** q   are all the family of 'g', etc.

Further aspects were noted. The students preferred the reading matter to be broken up into manageable chunks, and liked paragraphs that were well-defined by indenting and double spacing. Indented paragraphs were liked for the treatment of direct speech, as was the use of double quotation marks.

The illustrations used were considered more helpful if they preceded the printed matter to which they related, as they do in the *Oxford Pictorial Classics*, which, incidentally, also use Times Roman print.

Margins should be generous so the text does not appear to overfill the page and unjustified settings (that is, with a ragged edge to the right) should be used for adult non-readers so that an even word space is maintained. The same applies, obviously, to the disabled child reader.

Factors in the content

Factors in the content are again a matter of individual difference in the reader but publishers might pay attention to the fact that 'information' books are often preferred by the older disabled reader but few are produced with a sufficiently low reading age for them to be read with ease.

Factors in the language

Factors in the language or vocabulary have been the measure most used as a guide to readability as they lend themselves to being easily counted. That is, words – their length and rarity; the sentences, their length and degree of complexity, the ideas and concepts, the references and allusions to experience in common between writer and reader. But mostly these readability formulae involved words and sentences. They are nearly all of American origin and based on measures of word frequency, syllable load, repetition, sentence length and complexity within the selected sample from the text to be assessed.

Such formulae are often time consuming to apply and involve a considerable knowledge of formulae. For example:

• Dale and Chall readability formula (1948).
• Flesch (1948) 'A new readability yardstick'.
• Farr et al. (1951) 'Simplification of Flesch reading ease formula'.
• Fry (1968) 'A readability formula that saves time'.

Fry's Readability Graph is reasonably easy to use but is also American in origin. It has, however, been adapted and reproduced in the BBC Adult Literacy Handbook, pages 68–69, given as reading ages instead of grades.

A more recent attempt to assess the difficulty level of materials is given by Moyle (1971) in the Reading Curriculum, where the reader has to supply the word left out of the original passage – the Cloze Procedure.

Perhaps the simplest of all is that suggested by Johnson (1973) which he calls the Five Finger Test. He says:

- Choose the book you like.
- Open it near the middle.
- Try to find a page without pictures.
- Start reading at the top and go on until you come to a word you do not know.
- Put your little finger on it.
- Continue reading, putting a finger on every word you do not know until you run out of fingers.
- If you run out before you get to the bottom of the page the book is probably too difficult for you.

The idea is that most early stage books have about a hundred words to the page and if the reader is unable to read more than five words in every hundred it is unlikely that he will be able to read it without help.

A linguist's view is given by Granowsky and Botel (1974), who recognize the shortcomings in readability formulae and propose a technique for analysing syntatic complexity of texts. It is divided into *count structures*, which score 0, 1, 2 or 3, according to their complexity.

- The structures that count 0 are sentence patterns with two or three lexical items, e.g. subject – verb – object, etc.
- The structures that count 1 are sentence patterns with four lexical items, e.g. subject – verb – object – complement.
- The structures that count 2 are sentences containing passives, comparatives, infinitives as objects or as subjects, and so on.
- The structures that count 3 are sentences with clauses used as subjects and absolutes.

It will be seen, then, that all such methods, except Johnson's Five Finger Test are very time consuming and would seem to be outside the scope of a busy teacher's brief. It would be of great benefit to both teachers and pupils if publishers performed this task and stated both the reading age and interest age of books published for children to read, as well as paying attention to the typeface used and the attractiveness of the presentation.

Factors in the phonemic or phonetic structure

It is now firmly established by centres specializing in reading and spelling disabilities that there are some children who are unable to learn by the whole-word method, or who need phonetic analysis and synthesis skills to back up their limited sight word vocabulary. For them, totally phonetic reading material is required and the phonetic complexities that will be encountered at each stage need to be clearly stated either at the end of the book or preferably at the beginning. It is then possible to match the child to the text so that he will never be in a position of being 'unable to read the book in his hand' as he will never meet any sound/spelling correspondence that he has not been specifically taught.

So far, at our clinic, we have encountered only three sets of reading books that meet these requirements (which use Times Roman print incidentally) and these are the *Alpha to Omega* stories, the *Pam and Tom Reading Scheme*, published by Focus Trading (books one to nine), and the new *Alpha to Omega Fiction* (Birkbeck and Oxford 1999). The stories have been skilfully devised so that they are acceptable at all age levels and approximately five or six short stories of comparable difficulty are presented in each book.

Finally, since it was stated earlier that one of the aims of education was to create a literate population, perhaps it would not be inappropriate to quote from GM Trevelyan (*English Social History*, chapter 18), who said that 'Education has produced a vast population able to read but unable to distinguish what is worth reading.'

References

Birkbeck D, Oxford G (1999) *Alpha to Omega Fiction*. Oxford: Heinemann Educational.

Dale E, Chall JS (1948) A formula for predicting readability. *Educational Research Bulletin* **27**: 11–20, 37–54.

Farr JN, Jenkins JJ, Paterson DH (1951) Simplification of Flesch reading ease formula. *Journal of Applied Psychology* **32**(3): 221–33.

Flesch R (1948) 'A new readability yardstick'. Journals of Applied Psychology 35: 333–337.

Fry EA (1968) A readability formula that saves time. *Journal of Reading* **II**(7): 513–16.

Gilliland J (1972) *Readability*. London: University of London Press.

Granowsky, Botel (1974) Linguistic complexity formula. *The Reading Teacher* **28**(1).

Johnson TD (1973) Reading games and activities. *Reading* **7**(1): 4–10.

Moyle D (1971) Readability: the use of the cloze procedure. In *The Reading Curriculum* (ed Merritt). London: Ward Lock.

Paterson DG, Tinker MA (1940) *How to Make Type Readable*. New York: Harper and Brothers.

Peters M (1971) *Trends in Reading Schemes*. Cambridge: Institute of Education.

Sassoon R (1991) A typeface with a special purpose. *Linotype Letterbox* no. 6: 10–11.

Sassoon R (1983) *The Practical Guide to Children's Handwriting*. London: Thames & Hudson.

Walker S (1992) *How it Looks: research into typography*. Reading & Language Information Centre, Reading University.

Williamson H (1966) *Methods of Book Design*. Oxford: Oxford University Press.

CHAPTER 11

Those for whom the system has failed

JEAN JONES

> I'd sooner be an ordinary kid in a special school than a special kid in an ordinary school.
>
> (Michael, aged 15)

This very powerful statement was made to me during one of many very frank and open interviews concerning children's personal experiences of school and special education. I was collecting the views and opinions of children and young people as part of a small research study for the Wirral branch of the National Association for Special Educational Needs (NASEN) on how young people perceived their own difficulties, and the provision made to meet those needs. My original study covered a wide variety of difficulties and special needs but for the purposes of this book I shall confine the discussion to those with dyslexia or SLD (the term most favoured by educationalists on Wirral).

Such a profound comment speaks volumes and opens up the whole issue of how we listen and respond to the views of children, especially those with special educational needs. In the main, it is the viewpoint of adults that is the prime influence on discussions and debates about education, the curriculum and how schools are managed. As adults we may need to re-examine our own values and beliefs, particularly when it comes to actively seeking the views of children and young people and giving them real consideration. Generally it is adults who make all the decisions on behalf of young people, whether or not they are capable of making their own choices. It is our own (parents', teachers' and others') convictions and beliefs imposed on those we profess to care about.

Children are the subject of much testing and assessment, case conferences and general discussion, the outcome of which will be dependent on the views of the dominant adults (usually the professionals). Actions we, as adults, very arrogantly justify by claiming them to be 'in the best interests of the child'.

In this modern-day philosophy of 'market forces', children are central to the education system. Yet it is a variety of adults who are consulted, even though children and young people, being on the receiving end of services, are the real consumers. Children have to be educated, usually in schools, regardless of whether they enjoy it, or can cope, or succeed in such an environment. Children are afforded rights, yet have no power and rarely have any choice. If we do not like our jobs or the people we have to work and deal with we have the option of leaving and walking away. We tend not to afford our young people the same options.

We impose systems, strategies and an array of services on our children, yet we rarely take the trouble to ask them about their own thoughts and feelings. When we do, it is all too easy to dismiss those views, if they do not agree with our own, by claiming that they are too young, or don't understand, and that 'we know best'.

Consulting children in general, let alone special needs children, tends to receive low emphasis. By law, it is parents who are consulted about schools and the curriculum, not the child. For schools, ever conscious of government demands and the expectations of parents, it is easy to overlook the wishes and needs of their pupils.

Children have been given the right to be consulted through the legislative framework of the UN Convention, the Children Act and a succession of Education Acts. The Code of Practice that resulted from the 1993 Education Act provides a framework for involving the child. With more and more emphasis on inclusion and educating special needs children in mainstream classes, obtaining their views must become a priority if we are to significantly improve their learning opportunities.

Every child is important and in determining the questions to ask, we need to be aware of what children's needs (rather than just rights) are. How and to what extent they are met depends on ability as well as disability and can have wider implications, affecting social, family and educational settings.

To ascertain these needs the number of adults involved can vary from just a few to many. The child is then the subject of a variety of beliefs and value systems held by each of these individuals, thus affecting the provision offered. These opinions can probably be divided into three categories. There are those whose aim is to reduce or overcome the child's difficulties, some who take a preventive stand, and others who will support and maintain the child, treating their difficulties as ordinary. All will ask different questions and look at a different aspect of the child, based on the context of the service involved.

Opinions vary and provision often is as a result of compromise between all these viewpoints. In such circumstances it is difficult to see how the child at the centre of all this can ever have a voice when nobody is really prepared to listen. We are usually too busy deciding on 'what's best' to give proper consideration to asking the child for his or her own thoughts.

In trying to address some of these issues I undertook a small-scale study to look at the views of children with special educational needs. I deliberately did not have set questions or ideas but just let the children tell their own stories. Their views were very frank, open and honest. Of the 156 stories collected, 38 were from dyslexic children or young adults. Of these, 28 were boys and 10 were girls. In well over half of these youngsters their difficulties were not identified until late in their educational careers and some only after leaving school.

From these personal accounts roughly five areas of difficulty or criticism could be identified. These were:

- individual personal difficulties
- relationships with teachers
- relationships with other pupils
- the general attitude to school
- feelings about mainstream versus special education.

The personal difficulties talked about not only included their own innermost feelings but also how they outwardly portrayed themselves to others in developing coping and/or avoidance strategies. Eight of the youngsters talked about their feelings of isolation, of shame and embarrassment, as well as a feeling of having something to hide. Many viewed themselves negatively and felt inadequate alongside their peers. The views of one 16-year-old, Gareth, can be used to sum this up.

> I was ashamed in part, mostly it was the girls that skit. I'm lucky as far as having common (sense) because I could hide a lot of it. It's a big thing emotionally, if you can't cope people laugh at you. I can cope now because I learnt strategies. It was like climbing a ladder to wash windows and I can see in now.

Four youngsters reported feeling devalued and made to feel different, and labels seemed to play a large part in this. Many felt they were seen only in terms of the labels they had been given. Often these were considered to be wrong and hard to get rid of or overcome. Youngsters felt stigmatized by being called slow, or lazy, or even stupid. Some 21 children mentioned labels of this kind. Two children were actually accused of attention seeking. Twenty-four of the youngsters mentioned incidents of bullying, name calling, being picked on, teased or skitted.

> I was in the remedial class when they (teachers) first found out I had dyslexia. They said I was a slow learner. We were made to feel different when labelled. The special needs class was known as the slow class. Only I knew just how hard I was trying and how much I wanted to read.
>
> (Paul, aged 15)

> Labels are part of the problem. It makes it sound like a disease. We're not a problem but have difficulty with reading and writing.
>
> (Joanne, aged 14)

Not all youngsters felt this way, indeed two girls were quite relieved to have, as they saw it, a real reason for their inability to read and write. One saw the diagnosis of dyslexia as the key to her problems, as she now felt able to cope, knowing what was wrong and how to deal with it. Having previously been too ashamed to ask for help, and believing that being unable to read was something to hide, she felt her life had changed because she had found the reason behind her difficulties.

Many of these young people talked about their inability to cope and this frequently led to emotional distress, often leading to illness. This was both real and perceived, and a way of 'getting out of school or certain lessons'. A large proportion of the youngsters lacked confidence, believing their difficulties were their own fault and that there was something wrong with them. This inability to cope led to feelings of frustration, which manifested itself in anger and hatred directed at family, teachers and school.

Seventeen-year-old Anthony, whose mother discovered he was dyslexic, reports such feelings and emotions.

> I used to get angry, annoyed and frustrated. I knew what I wanted to write but couldn't get it out or down on paper. I'd get confused and my confidence was affected. I was accused of being thick, or soft, or daft. My frustrations would come out at home. I would cry and batter my pillows. This usually resulted from an accumulation of things.

Sixteen-year-old Gareth made similar comments.

> I was angry most of the time, at the teachers, at authority. The teachers put me down. I used to say to myself, why can't I do it? Other kids can do it. I couldn't understand myself. Some teachers wouldn't let me in their lessons.

Twenty of the youngsters admitted to engaging in some kind of difficult or disruptive behaviour and seven actually admitted to truanting. Nigel was one of these pupils and was quite matter-of-fact about his school attendance. Nigel now successfully runs his own small business.

I never used to go to school every day because some of the lessons didn't really interest me and some of the teachers I didn't really get on with. The lessons I used to enjoy, yes, these were worth going to. I'd go there and take part in the lesson, be an active part in it, but certain lessons and certain teachers, it wasn't worth the hassle going there. I didn't really dislike school, I didn't stay away because of problems at home or anything like that. It's just if there's a problem at home you don't go home, if there's a problem at school you don't go to school. My mum knew I was playing truant but she wasn't able to do anything really. I'd set off for school and by the time I got there I'd be late, then I'd think – oh it's not worth the hassle going in because I'm late. So I didn't.

Several youngsters had developed coping strategies that relied heavily on the help and support of family and friends who would copy or do work for them. In most cases, this type of support eventually broke down, or failed, or was removed by such means as being separated from classmates. As a result, most developed some form of emotional and/or behavioural difficulties similar to those already described.

Here on Wirral we are fortunate to have a maintained special school, Orretts Meadow, that caters primarily for primary-aged children with SLDs. There are, on average, only 60 places in the school and it is always heavily oversubscribed. This tends to be top heavy with year five and six pupils, the majority of whom are boys. This indicates a possible lateness in identifying the needs of some children.

The Code of Practice on the Identification and Assessment of Special Educational Needs, places great importance on early identification. Wirral's Policy Statement incorporates this principle by saying:

Children who have special educational needs should be identified at the earliest possible stage and appropriate provision determined.

One of the fundamental principles of the Code of Practice states that:

...the needs of all pupils who may have special educational needs either throughout, or at any time during, their school careers must be addressed

Wirral's policy document goes on to say that:

There should be a coherent continuum of provision and services to ensure that the appropriate expertise, resources and curricular practice become routinely available to all pupils with special educational needs.

This policy document was adopted in 1991 by Wirral Education Committee, before the advent of the Code of Practice. The authority was at that time very forward-thinking in that it had developed a Special Needs Handbook, which was based on a five-stage procedure, not dissimilar to that recommended by the Code. This specialist provision at primary level also offers an outreach service to dyslexic children (approximately two, one-and-a-quarter hour sessions per week in their school) who have been unable to obtain a place in the school. At secondary level there is the Sanderling Unit, within the grounds of a mainstream secondary school. This unit caters for approximately 40 pupils of at least average ability with SLDs. These children usually have additional problems, such as social and emotional difficulties. This school also takes pupils with other problems, such as Asperger's syndrome.

Looking at all this, one could be forgiven for thinking that dyslexic pupils on Wirral were well catered for. My experience of the education system and trying to get the appropriate resources to meet my dyslexic son Paul's needs proved otherwise. This view is supported by the many stories and experiences I come across in my role as a parent supporter.

Paul was treated very much as a slow learner and one psychologist actually intimated that he was 'backward'. One of his teachers made the comment that if we had lived in downtown Birkenhead (we are fortunate enough to live in what is commonly known as 'the leafy suburbs' and an 11-plus area), then he wouldn't have been noticeable!

Knowing that there was something wrong, but not agreeing with the professional interpretation of my son's difficulties, I began to investigate learning difficulties for myself and this led to my subsequent and further interest and involvement in special educational needs.

Having discovered dyslexia through my many hours of reading in the local library, I had to pay for a private assessment in order to confirm the diagnosis. It was through my own investigations into provision and resources that I discovered the specialist school Orretts Meadow. It took two years of arguing and wrangling with the local authority to first get them to assess and then to complete the procedures. To achieve this I twice had to complain to the Secretary of State and the Local Ombudsman. By this time my son was 'too old' to attend the specialist school.

All this happened some 13 years ago, and I fear little has changed. In many cases, dyslexia is still discovered by the parents initially, and all too frequently this is heavily dependent on their ability to pay for private assessments.

One particular family that I have supported for the past 18 months have, after much procrastination with the Education Department, eventually had their son's difficulties recognized, acknowledged and catered for. They were finally offered a part-time placement in Orretts Meadow (five mornings per week) just days before schools closed for the summer holidays. In agreeing to this offer, the parents were influenced by the fact that Zack will be a year six pupil in September. As it is so late in his primary education his parents had to give consideration to the fact that any further disagreement and prolonged negotiation with the local authority could limit the duration of Zack's access to this specialist provision before having to move on to secondary school. Provision at secondary level is very much restricted to the provision individual mainstream schools make for pupils with special educational needs. Much of the success in obtaining Zack's Statement and achieving some provision was dependent on his parents' determination, energy and, most importantly, their ability to pay for several private reports and engage a specialist private tutor.

The implementation of the Code of Practice was intended to facilitate the early identification and assessment of special needs, but the government's squeeze on spending over many years has led to cuts in education budgets. While Wirral is justifiably proud of their achievement in maintaining schools' budgets, the same cannot be said for the funding of central services such as learning support and the educational psychology service. Both of these services have seen a large reduction in staff and have subsequently amalgamated as one service.

As from September 1997, Wirral schools can no longer access psychological involvement for any child at stage three of the procedures for a learning difficulty. This is now the remit of the learning support service. This is a team of specialist teachers whose role is to work with the special needs co-ordinators (SENCOs) in designing individual education programmes for children with learning difficulties. Some, but not all, of these teachers have a Diploma in Specific Learning Difficulties and, on average, visit schools every two or three weeks. Not all children will be seen or discussed during these visits. Some schools will have a higher incidence of learning difficulties and, due to time allocation restrictions of this service, they have to prioritize children. While the support service work involves diagnostic assessment, there is no direct teaching carried out by these specialists. Any additional individual specialist teaching can only come via a Statement.

Such processes and procedures have the unfortunate consequence of children with dyslexia not being identified early enough and so frequently missing out on obtaining the very specialist teaching they need in order to progress and experience educational success. Wirral has set criteria governing the movement between the stages and in effect what this means is that young people have to reach a certain level of failure before they can access a system that may bring them some additional specialist help and support. Due to the increasing numbers of children of primary level who would benefit from access to either the specialist school or the outreach work offered, this is also governed by certain criteria.

Under such a system, if a parent or teacher suspects that a child may be dyslexic there is little chance of this being diagnosed or officially recognized before stage four of the procedures (formal assessment), unless the parents have the financial means to obtain a private psychological report.

It is easy to see how under such a system dyslexia can be termed as a 'middle-class' disease. Parents need stamina, persistence and confidence, as well as good oral and written abilities to make a strong case to the school and/or education authority. This often needs to be backed up by evidence that can be provided only if parents have the financial ability to obtain private assessments and tuition. Some parents are disadvantaged in that they are less able to present and argue their case for a variety of reasons, not least of which may be that they have learning difficulties themselves. This obviously creates major equal opportunities issues for both the parent and the child.

Wirral's ability to provide for children with SLDs within both mainstream and special education allowed me to make some useful comparisons between the way children are educated in the two settings. Of the 38 children who participated in my study, 12 were educated in a totally mainstream setting, 21 moved from mainstream to special, two moved back from special to mainstream during their primary career (in Wirral the majority of children move back into mainstream on transfer to secondary education), two children started off in special education and one child moved to private education.

Relationships featured quite heavily and focused on those between pupil and pupil, and those between teacher and pupil. Relationships for children in special educational settings seemed more stable and acceptable, because, as one child said, 'the other kids usually have problems like you' (Melanie, aged 9, special school).

The relationships with other pupils in mainstream schools featured much of what has already been described, such as name calling, teasing, skitting and bullying, as well as staff and other pupils not understanding the problems and difficulties dyslexics face.

The feeling of being made to feel different featured in the relationships with both other pupils and with teachers, and again there was a marked distinction between those children in special education and those in mainstream schools. The teachers in mainstream schools could be divided into the sympathetic and the unsympathetic. Those teachers described as unsympathetic were accused of lacking in patience, not having sufficient time to explain things and help the pupil through tasks, and lacking under-standing of a pupil's individual needs. Comments such as 'they write nasty things in your book like your handwriting is scruffy, you didn't listen and you could try harder' tended to have a very demoralizing effect on performance. As too did comments such as 'you read it there, why can't you read it here?' or 'you did it yesterday why can't you do it today?'. Most felt that these teachers had a very negative attitude and low expectations of pupils with difficulties. The majority of pupils could recall instances of being told by teachers that they were lazy, stupid or naughty. As far as schoolwork went, many felt that the only acceptable way of doing things had to be the teacher's way.

> Our group was picked on by some teachers. We were quite disruptive. We used to disrupt the class basically. We just had a bit too much lip for our own good, or so the teacher thought. We didn't do it in all the classes. Classes that really interested us we'd be OK in. Some of the maths interested us, some of it we'd done before so we'd think there's no point. When we wanted to do certain exams (GCSEs) the teacher said 'I don't think you've got the ability to do it', and we thought oh well if you're not going to give us the chance. I wasn't too happy about it. It affected my confidence badly and I didn't go to the exam.
>
> (Nigel, aged 22)

Some teachers were considered to be too sympathetic, making youngsters feel they were 'being treated like a baby' or as if 'you will get hurt', 'they feel sorry for you'. Other teachers were seen as interfering too much, not allowing sufficient time to 'work things out for yourself'.

Those pupils fortunate enough to have the benefit of individual specialist teaching or other support, or some individual time and tuition from the class teacher, were often made to feel like the teacher's pet. Others viewed their support workers as overprotective, affecting their social relationships because other pupils often wouldn't make approaches while an adult was constantly around. A small proportion of the youngsters did admit to sometimes depending on this support too much.

Those pupils who experienced special school education felt that teachers in this setting had more time to work with pupils and nearly always explained things better. These teachers were often viewed as kinder and more understanding. Several of the mainstream boys talked about how they had been 'turned around' by the interest and attention shown to them by a particular teacher. Fifteen-year-old Andrew had nothing but praise for one of his teachers.

> I then got this most amazing teacher ever. He took me out of the remedial class and brought me on leaps and bounds. He treated me like a person. Without him I'd have got nowhere, I had a total lack of motivation. His lessons mattered, I'd go in just for his lesson. He kept pushing for the best and if it hadn't been for him I'd have left long ago. He put his trust in the class and the class worked for him.

Of those children and young people who had experience of both mainstream and special school, I was surprised to find just how many actually preferred the special setting. On the whole, it was those pupils who had experienced Wirral's provision for children with SLD who were most positive about the experience. Some of the most common statements made included 'in special school you're the same as the others', 'you don't get bullied as much or teased, skitted or names called', 'the teachers have more understanding', 'the classes are smaller so the teachers have more time to explain things'.

In contrast, the reported views of those children and young people who had only experienced mainstream education was that 'the teachers have less time', 'it was harder to work and concentrate' and 'there are too many distractions'.

> I need peace and quiet to work. I still can't work in a classroom situation.
>
> (Mark, aged 14)

> ...the real trouble starts at secondary school. They are too big and there is too much pressure. The work is much harder and the teachers have less time.
>
> (Paul, aged 15)

The two children who moved from mainstream to special school and back again had the added difficulty coping successfully with the transfer. Greg said he felt 'out of step' with what was going on in the mainstream school. Both children felt they were not prepared for the change and found every-thing, from the size of the school and the classes to the work, extremely difficult to cope with. They felt they had to work harder and received less time from the teachers and 'I had to rely on other kids for help' (Simon, aged 13).

There were a few children whose experience of special education was that of a special needs class attached to a mainstream school. These children liked the smaller class sizes and the respite it provided from the demands of mainstream education, but the criticism was made that the work was often too easy. This comment was also echoed by those children in mainstream schools who had been in classes streamed for ability. Due to the way in which their needs and difficulties were viewed, many were placed in lower-ability classes.

From this small-scale study it can be seen that children's and young people's views and experiences can be quite varied. How we approach special needs and the provisions we make to meet them should reflect the diversity of need, including an individual's ability to grow and develop in different settings. The opportunity afforded to young people to gain maximum benefit from resources is heavily influenced by the strongly overriding principles, opinions and processes imposed by adults.

A natural progression of this study would be to follow the children's and young people's progress at GCSE exam level and on into adult life. My study used a very open design and, as such, the information obtained was very much centred on the issues that children and young people identified as important to themselves. Such a survey, while not as academic as most standard research studies, can provide a starting point for looking at issues about school and education that are of importance to children and young people.

Very few of the youngsters contributing to my study talked in any depth about exams such as GCSEs, or qualifications in general. Fifteen of the children in the study were not that far advanced in their secondary education career so it would be difficult to determine their long-term educational future.

Two young people, after achieving low-grade passes at GCSE level, went on to youth training schemes. One has gone on to successfully start up and run his own small business. The other is my son. In his total lack of belief in himself as a learner and his shame and embarrassment of having a learning difficulty, he would not admit to being dyslexic. This meant that his instructors did not identify and understand his learning needs. As a result he was constantly downgraded in his training, going from learning a trade to menial and labouring jobs. Each time this happened it reinforced his own negative view of himself and further damaged his already fragile self-esteem.

Paul managed to remain in employment for about four years after leaving school and, although he cannot see it, managed to achieve some success. One example of this is that he learnt to successfully get himself about the Wirral and Liverpool area using public transport – a task he was always very reticent to attempt. Paul has worked mostly on short-term contracts and unfortunately as each job finished he took it as a personal reflection on his ability. When his last employment finished in September 1997 it was the final straw in what he perceived to have been a long line of failures and he more or less gave up on himself and has been unemployed since.

Seven young people had their difficulties identified only after leaving school. Of those, four eventually joined adult literacy classes. Three of these had completed studies up to GCSE level and at the time of the study one man, Anthony, was part way through studying for a degree. He put this success down to the help, encouragement and support of his partner. The university too provided a lot of help and support. This man had spent many years avoiding anything to do with writing, using a variety of strategies to get others to complete written tasks for him. He even went as far as changing jobs to avoid people finding out about his difficulties with reading and writing.

In her recounting of her difficulties, 25-year-old Carol summed up such struggles quite clearly:

> I knew I had difficulties that other children didn't seem to have and I managed to hide my handicap for over 10 years. As I got older I felt increasingly isolated and became unable to cope with simple daily things like getting the bus or train and I was too ashamed to ask for help. It was a relief at being told there was a reason for my difficulties. The explicit teaching I received in the adult literacy classes brought me up to GCSE standards.

Based on this success and her new found confidence, Carol was planning to go on and learn to type.

Only one person went on to do A levels and although at the time of the study his grades were unknown, both he and his teachers expected him to do well. Examination opportunities and success were not mentioned by four of the respondents.

In four cases it was the child or young person's mother who was credited with recognizing their difficulties and arranging for private assessments to confirm a diagnosis of dyslexia. Of these, three of the children needed great persuasion to attend private specialist teaching. Seventeen-year-old Ian described how he hated school and didn't want anything to do with school or teachers as he didn't believe they would ever be able to help him.

> I was persuaded by my parents to have special lessons and I gradually realized that there were other kids with the same problem and I was not on my own. The teachers at the Institute are kind and no one can say you're thick because you're all the same. I am quite proud of my achievements and feel I am now making a success of my career (employment with a local retailer). Without the special help I would have left school bitter and frustrated with little reading and writing skills.

Wirral is fortunate enough to have an active Dyslexia Association. This group has made great strides over the past few years to try to redress this balance. They run a very successful resource centre in conjunction with the Central Library. A wide range of reading materials on dyslexia, children's books and teaching materials have been purchased and are available on loan through the library lending system. Through membership of the Association parents have access to other material, such as games and spell checkers.

A large donation from a local company enabled the Association to buy a computer and install it in the International Business Centre, or IBC as it is more generally known. Adult dyslexics now have access to this informaion technology equipment and can call on help from staff in the college. It is all part of the aim of getting adult dyslexics who have perhaps been failed by the system back into education or at least an educational setting.

Apart from providing parents with a helpline based in the library, support and help is offered in other ways. Talks and presentations are given on a variety of subjects. The Wirral Association also run a very successful adult support group, which offers help, support and a listening ear to people who are, or have been, unable to talk about their difficulties.

One gentleman, Tom, who was befriended as a result of seeking advice about his own son's difficulties, has gone on to be very successful. As an adult dyslexic he has been enabled to tackle his own difficulties and return to adult education. Last year he was successfully awarded Student of the Year, was instrumental in having the computer based in the college and now takes a leading role in the management of the resource base.

We should not presume to speak accurately for our children. We need to listen to what they say, to hear what really matters and is significant to them. Their views and experiences can show how well schools are working and contribute to the organization of provision. The insight offered by children and young people can have significant implications not only on teaching styles and classroom management but also on policy formation and the way the education system is organized.

An interesting quote taken from Musgrove (1964) says 'Children's biggest problem is not with their disability but the handicap created by adults and society'. This is probably as true today as it was then.

As a society, we tend to judge people on their ability to read and write. If you cannot manage this basic skill then the assumption all too often is that you are of lower intelligence. Success is measured by economics and in order to get the high-powered, high-paying jobs we need qualifications, qualifications obtained through the ability to use the written word. Placing such importance on an individual's ability to read and write devalues not only their other skills and talents but also their worth as an individual.

Reference

Musgrove (1964) *Youth and Social Order.*

CHAPTER 12

Selected case studies

The story of Trevor Atherton, written by himself

Trevor found his way to Bart's Hospital in 1974, at the age of 18, with a spelling age of 7. He was taught by Jane Taylor, who sent me the following extract, which he had written for the London Dyslexia Association. Trevor has also written a complete book, which is available to anyone who would like a copy. Unfortunately, we have been unable to contact Trevor as both he and his parents have moved and cannot be traced, but as he has already published his story in the *Newsletter of the London Dyslexia Association* I am sure he would not mind it being reproduced here.

Trevor's story

I am not an expert on dyslexia but I am an expert on being dyslexic. I am and always have been dyslexic. But I did not realize this until I was 17, in fact almost 18. It was my ex-boss who realized my problem, his patience having been tried so many times by customers sending back various forms full of spelling mistakes and demanding to know the reason why. How fortunate that my ex-boss took the trouble to investigate the reasons for my dreadful spelling and writing and did not just dismiss me.

Finding out that I was dyslexic was a very traumatic experience. I had no idea what it was or how I came to get it. Did you just catch it? There was no one to ask; in fact, no one seemed to know anything about it. I had to find out for myself. I had a lot of help from my mother who all through my schooldays had believed in me and insisted that I was not stupid which was the label I was given, and had tried to get help and advice from school staff but without any success. I did eventually find out what dyslexia meant but I had to wait a long time before I could get any help. It took numerous telephone calls to hospitals, clinics, etc. to find out where there were remedial courses for people like myself, but finally, I got an appointment at St Bartholomew's hospital with a specialist and had to undergo various tests before being pronounced dyslexic. I was still very confused about the whole thing, but I did feel comforted that at last a very real reason had been found for my slowness at school and that I was not the stupid boy I had been labelled all through my schooldays. There was a definite thing wrong and what is more, I could learn to overcome it. I was immediately referred to the dyslexic clinic at St Bartholomew's and I attended there every week for more than two years. It was hard tedious work, but I had a lot of help and encouragement.

I would like to describe something of my schooldays and what it meant to be dyslexic in the 1960s and early 1970s. In spite of my disability, I enjoyed school which is surprising as I was always being told I was lazy or just plain silly. No one ever thought to question why I appeared to be these things. No one said, this boy does have a brain what is wrong, what is preventing him from learning? No, as far as the teachers were concerned, I was given a label and left to get on as best I could. When I was 16, I felt ready to leave school. School staff and career officers alike considered the best place for me was in a factory or warehouse where I didn't have to think. If only they had known, how my brain ached to be used and already I knew that I wanted to work with people not machinery.

At the age of 15, I managed to learn to read and when I left school having just reached 17, I had absolutely no future. I had several jobs before going to the one where my boss bothered to look beyond obvious and suggested to me that I might be dyslexic. I eventually left my job there and went to work in a hospital as a porter; it was a start towards my ambition to work with people who needed help and care. I was able to continue my studies with St Bartholomew's and it was hard going, but I didn't mind, as now at last, I could see the light ahead. I continued working as a hospital porter until I finished at St Bartholomew's. Then came the biggest step in my life. At last, I could step out of the slot I had been put into at school and I went into nursing where I could do what I had always wanted to do. I completed a two-year SEN training for mentally handicapped people and I am now a teacher for the mentally handicapped in a day centre.

I am still dyslexic. I always will be. But it doesn't matter now. I know what it is. I have faced up to it and accepted it. It is a fight being dyslexic. I have fought to get where I am. I have thrown off my 'stupid' label of my schooldays and I am now a working member of a team of specialized people in the day centre where I work. To all dyslexics, I would say: don't let people push you under the table or to one side. Be proud of what you are. Ask if you cannot spell a word. I do. If you really want to overcome this handicap, you can. But it is up to you, only you can do it.

Jason's story, written by his mother

As the mother of a dyslexic child I thought it would be appropriate to make some comments from my perspective, having anxiously witnessed my son's struggles over the years and the consequent ramifications for our family. Jason is my second child. His sister was born in Tanzania (East Africa) nearly four years earlier. She was always popular with her teachers, being a bright, co-operative child, interested in her schoolwork. Their father is a Greek national brought up in East Africa who speaks, reads and writes three languages.

Jason was born in England, officially 10 days late, after an induced labour and forceps delivery. The labour was comparatively short, but the contractions started to fade away before he was delivered, hence the forceps. His birthweight was 8 lb 4oz and after delivery he was bed-rested for 24 hours – nobody touched him – due to his stressful birth. After our return to East Africa he was breast-fed for seven, trouble-free months. But then I started him on cow's milk, which was more easily available than imported tinned milk. This made him very colicky.

As a small child, Jason was always bright, amusing, confident and exceptionally well co-ordinated. He could walk before he was a year old. His first steps were literally that – he walked away from me one morning when I set him down. Certainly he was mischievous and infuriating as all small children can be, but had great powers of concentration and was extremely dextrous with his favourite Lego construction toys. Learning to eat with a spoon, tying shoelaces, ball games and swimming all came easily to him.

From two years of age he went to a playgroup and amazed his rather strict 'teacher' with his ability to place different sizes of beans neatly and symmetrically round a piece of play dough, even though he preferred hanging upside down on the climbing frame to doing as instructed.

He started school at five, where his troubles began. Although his young, English expatriate teacher was extremely kind, she was not bothered at his lack of learning, merely suggesting 'a bit of help' at home. I thought it very odd that he just couldn't learn to read. His sister had never had any problems with learning to read and I could read well by the time I was six.

Not only could Jason barely read by the time he was 10, but also his handwriting was atrocious and his spelling was imaginative to say the least. He was constantly in trouble at school for his aggression and lack of attention in the classroom and was once accused of bullying a smaller child. I was shocked at this and made a point of seeking out his accuser who did actually back down. One teacher could not deal with him at all and made him stand outside the classroom. The school decided his problem was not a problem at all as they had 40 different nationalities and they all had to cope in an English teaching medium, not seeming to realize that Jason's first, and only, language was English! His confidence was severely tried. However, some teachers tried to help and he was sent for remedial lessons. Only one teacher realized how bright he was when, at nine years old, he was the only member of the class who could remember from the end of one term to the beginning of the next exactly what the class had been reading the previous term and which part of the book. The school librarian told me that Jason enjoyed library sessions, was never disruptive and always chose books with engineering diagrams

By this time I had decided he was rather stupid, although I knew that this could not be true of someone who could converse with eloquence and relate long complicated 'jokes' very skilfully. Eventually a friend suggested he might be dyslexic. I was dismayed by this news but arranged for him to be tested at a Dyslexic Institute in Staines. Jason refused to co-operate with most of the tests and no conclusive results could be obtained. The final report suggested that 'Jason would do what he wanted when he wanted'.

Socially it was very difficult for Jason because he was considered to be aggressive and disruptive. His reputation preceded him and some people were hostile to him before they had even met him. The suggestion that he might have learning difficulties such as dyslexia was met with comments such as 'a fashionable excuse'. I had to witness his embarrassment and struggles with books he could not read and felt quite despairing. Eventually, I decided he would never get the help he needed in East Africa and set about finding a suitable boarding school in England.

This was not easy due to his poor academic record and he was now 10 years old. He was accepted by a prep school in the West country, but I was pleased when he was accepted at age 11 by the Oratory Junior School, near Reading. When I thanked the headmaster for giving Jason a chance, he told me that they had tests designed to show any kind of potential even if the child had done nothing but climb trees. This school was Jason's salvation because the remedial teacher, Mrs Patience Thomson, realized that Jason's problems needed thorough identification. She recommended that Dr Bevé Hornsby be consulted.

Dr Hornsby was the first person to give my son hope and tell him how clever he was and she asked him if would he prefer Oxford or Cambridge University at a later stage. His smile of pleasure at this question still remains with me. When he saw his high IQ scores, he told me he wanted to wear a badge at school saying 'I am not stupid and can prove it'.

Jason did have other problems. He was, and still is, allergic to cow's milk. It makes his pulse race, causes a blocked nose and we all knew when on exeats (half-term holiday), he had indulged himself in a milkshake! He also had an eye problem, which caused him to turn his head to try to read, which was noticed by Dr Hornsby at his first interview. Fortunately the Royal Berkshire Hospital had a special unit dealing with eye problems for children with learning difficulties and he was taken on as a patient. Jason did all his eye exercises regularly and within three months the eye problem was corrected and his reading skills, under Mrs Thomson's tutelage, improved dramatically.

Just before Jason was due to sit his GCE O levels, a test at the Hornsby Centre revealed a difficulty with reading black writing on white paper. He was referred to the Irlen Institute for investigation. After rigorous eye tests he was prescribed spectacles with a particular shade of blue lenses, which were acquired just in time for the O-level examinations. He achieved 10 O-level passes: two at A grade, four at B grade and four at C grade His confidence improved considerably and after this he never looked back, particularly as a registered dyslexic he could now have 25% extra time for exams! He gained three passes at A level, scoring ABB, and was accepted at Birmingham University for the BA(Hons) degree in Commerce. He left last year with a 2:1 degree and is currently employed by ING Barings in the City of London.

There still remains the problem of short-term memory. According to experimental evidence, short-term memory lasts for 6–15 seconds before being encoded into long-term memory. One of the problems with children like Jason is that short-term memory does not seem to exist at all. Unless they immediately write down information, and I am thinking particularly of telephone situations, they seem to have no recall. Many is the time that Jason has exasperated members of his family by not passing on telephone messages because he thinks he will remember the message, does not bother to write it down and of course he fails.

Despite the academic success, Jason's spelling is still erratic and the memories of embarrassment and derision remain with him. He will not use his blue-lens glasses at work and neither will he let anyone know of his dyslexia when his written reports are poor. He is angry with me when I suggest that perhaps his colleagues would admire him if they knew what he copes with. He sees his dyslexia as a stigma, something to be ashamed of, setting him apart from others and tantamount to being moronic. Such is the lack of understanding in our society even in these enlightened days. Not all his teachers at secondary school were sympathetic either – even though they knew his problem. One of his English teachers was the worst offender and 'corrected' a beautifully presented piece of work with red Biro all over the page. She also became frustrated with him in the classroom and commented, 'Jason why can't you be like everyone else'. Jason coolly told her, 'Because I am not like everyone else'. When Jason was faced with the questionnaire from the Hornsby Centre he said, 'Well this is one form I don't have to worry about the spelling!'

I would like to conclude this rather long comment by expressing the hope that Dr Hornsby's book be par for student teachers on teacher training courses, particularly those intending to teach at primary level, and recommended reading for everyone else in the profession. My son has dealt with his problems with courage and imagination but thank goodness for computers and particularly spell checkers. Fortunately for Jason and our family, we were in a position to pay for the extra professional help he needed. I often wonder what happens to those children who remain undiagnosed for economic reasons and therefore do not receive the specialist tuition they need. I shudder to think what would have happened to my son in this situation. Would he have been considered unteachable and eventually unemployable? It is clear from his academic achievement that he is very intelligent. He is also physically very strong and energetic, and I think about how he might have dissipated his energy and used his considerable intellect. Fortunately I do not have to answer that question.

The story of Charles Tillet

Charles's story is taken from his own response to our questionnaire and from his CV – also prepared by himself. It is taken directly from his script, including the occasional spelling error.

Was it a relief when you were told that you were dyslexic, or did it worry you?
It never really made any difference to me because in my one mind it meant nothing, I was still the same as before and still finding everything frostratingly hard even to achieve a substandard grade. It seemed to me their as it still dose now that when it came down to it that, no matter how high people say your IQ is or how intelligent you would have been if you were not burdened with this 'upper class disease' you are still less attractive to a potential employer than someone with higher grades and lower IQ.

Did you have any special help after your assessment? If so what? Was it helpful?
I had about seven years of extra English lessons mostly with a lady called Ann Holly, which seemed to help me a great deal but was still a real struggle which in my eyes did not dramatically improve my spelling, but this is probably just because I ant still making mistakes to this day and need a computer to achieve an expectable standard of writing. If I look at the grades I achieved in GCSE English it goes to show that these lessons must have helped vastly because there is no way I could have ever got those grades by myself.

What was school like before you knew that you were dyslexic? Did anything change afterwards? Be as frank and open as possible
This was all a long lime ago for me but some of the memories have stuck until this day. Even after I had been diagnosed there seemed to he no real hope for the future, it seemed as if I was no good at anything. Because I always used to compare myself with my friends around me, which I am sure all children and even adults do, who at worst seemed to be good at something but mostly good at everything. There is still some small line of thought which nags at me to this day which tells me that everyone around is better but now I know that this is not always the case.

There is a poem which came to inspire me over recent years which has just kept on proving itself and is very appropriate, it is by anonymous writer:

If you think you are beaten you are,
If you think you dare not, you don't,
If you'd like to win, but you think you can't
It's almost certain you won't,
If you think you'll lose, you've lost,
For out of all the world we find
Success begins with a fellows will –
It's all in the state of mind.
If you think your outclassed, you are,
You've got to think high to rise
You've got to be sure of yourself before
You can ever win a prize.
Life's battles do not always go
To the stronger or faster man,
But sooner or later the man who wins
Is the one who thinks he can.

What are you doing now?
I have just finished my first week at Reading University which is promising to be both very rewarding academically as well as socially, everyone hear seems to just like you for who you are as opposed to what the image lays down that you should be. I am studying a four year coarse in Land Management with a diploma in Urban Planning hoping to become a Chartered Surveyor at the end of it all.

The interval between finishing at school and starting at university has been predominantly taken up with rowing. After having completed a number of trials, the most testing lime of my life, I somehow got selected to row in the junior world championships, which I found to be an unparalleled experience.

Charles Tillet as a young man.

Is your dyslexia affecting what you are doing now? If so, what difficulties are you experiencing? For example your work or student life, and your social or sex life? As far as I am concerned the only way dyslexia is affecting me now that I have slopped receiving help is in a very positive way. Know that dyslexia is so wall recognised and relatively well understood by the general population allowances are made such as being given hours of extra time to do exams as well as subsidies for computers and understanding staff who realise that you are not either stupid or lazy.

EDUCATION

Marlborough House School
Hawkhurst
Kent   1983–1991

Shrewsbury School
Shropshire   1991–1996

EXAMINATIONS

GCSE

English language	C	English literature	B	Maths	B
Physics	C	Chemistry	C	Biology	C
Geography	B	French	D	Classical	B
Design & technology	B			civilization	

GCE A level

Biology	C	Geography	C	Ancient history	B

English Speaking Board Examination,   Credit

Two questionnaires

Two contrasting questionnaires as written by the people in question. Unfortunately they are anonymous.

Please answer the following questionnaire as fully and frankly as possible. If need be, continue any answer on a separate sheet.

What made you decide to refer your son/daughter for an educational assessment?

> AT SUGGESTION OF HIS SCHOOL

Did you seek special help for your son/daughter after the assessment? If so, what?

> YES. SPECIAL TEACHING ARRANGED BY SCHOOL.

Was it helpful?

> NO

Did you notice any change in your son/daughter academically, behaviourally and emotionally?

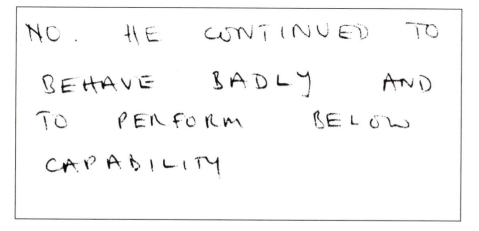

> NO. HE CONTINUED TO BEHAVE BADLY AND TO PERFORM BELOW CAPABILITY

Were you encouraged by the special help your son/daughter received after the assessment?

NO

Did the school's attitude change once your son/daughter was diagnosed as dyslexic?

NO

Do you have any further comments. For example on the diagnosis and treatment of your son/daughter and how you and he/she coped.

In retrospect would you change anything you did?

Please answer the following questions as fully as possible making any amusing or unpleasant comments that you think would be interesting. Please continue any answer on a separate sheet if need be.

Was it a relief when you were told that you were dyslexic, or did it worry you?

I was told that I was dyslexic at 6½, so I think I just accepted the fact, just as one accepts one's eye colour. Because I was diagnosed so early, by the time I was able to comprehend the possible limitations that being dyslexic can produce I had started to overcome the problem and so was not unduly disturbed by the idea.

Did you have any special help after your assessment? If so, what?

I was lucky enough to have lessons on a weekly basis for the next 5 yrs with a private teacher. The lessons were productive because my parents had the time and inclination to reinforce the rules and patterns I was learning outside the lessons.

Was this helpful?

By the time I was 11, as I had stopped having lessons because I had managed to overcome the problem sufficiently to manage fine at school.

What was school like - before you knew you were dyslexic? Did anything change afterwards? Be as frank and open as possible.

I really cannot remember a time before I knew I was dyslexic. After my diagnosis and extra lessons the improvements in the my language skills was slow and steady, but I never found that dyslexia was handicapping me in my schoolwork. Perhaps this was not only due to the extra lessons raising to tackle the problem, but also because my junior school was a very caring environment, where my bad spelling was accepted without humiliating me and the *

Did you get any GCSE's or 'O'- Levels? If so, how many and what grades?

I have 10 GCSE's all of which are A grades.

* improvements welcomed. By the time I started GCSE's were the need for language skills went to school I was managing to cope like anyone else, virtually.

Did you get any 'A'-Levels? If so, which subjects and what grades?

I did Biology - Grade A and Step Biology Grade 1
Chemistry - Grade A
Physics - Grade B.

Did you go to university?

Yes, I am currently studying medicine at Trinity Hall Cambridge.

What are you doing now?

I am about to enter my 3rd year at university, and am completing the year doing an e.g. the equivalent of a BA in Pathology.

Is your dyslexia affecting what you are doing now? If so, what difficulties are you experiencing? For example your work or student life, and your social and sex life!!

I don't feel that my dyslexia is hampering me now, at all really. All my university exams are done with no extra time and this has not really affected me since last year I got a II.i. At school + university friends all knew about my dyslexia and simply accept it as a facet of my personality, very few realise the effort that various people put in to *

Do you have any further comments? For example; on how you were diagnosed and treated or how you have coped with dyslexia or any entertaining stories which Beve can use in her book.

My diagnosis was dependent on the careful observations my teachers made of me at school, without which my extra lessons would have started later and perhaps not have been as fruitful - for this I am very grateful. I was also lucky that the educational climate in which I grew up was very supportive of the individual and I never experienced any teasing or nasty comments - a fact I am also grateful for. *

* help me overcome the problem and enable me to have a chance to fulfil my potential.

Adrian Fordham

This young man was one of the first patients who came to Bart's Hospital Dyslexia Clinic and came all the way from Norfolk every week. He appeared in the QED programme *I'm brighter than you think.*

Questionnaire for parents

Name: Anne and Michael Fordham
Name/names of child/children: Adrian Fordham 11.05.1971 Student
Clare Fordham 24.06.1973 Teacher

Please answer the following questions as fully as possible, making amusing or anecdotal comments wherever appropriate

Was it a relief when your child was diagnosed dyslexic?   Yes

At least the problem had been identified and we were able to seek the appropriate help for Adrian. Easier said than done, but we will always be very grateful for the tremendous support as well as excellent teaching we received from Bart's Dyslexia Clinic.

Did anybody's attitude change? Child, school, siblings, yourself?

Not really. If anything, the school and LEA became even more hostile to us. I am relieved to say the attitude of the LEA has improved beyond all recognition in the last few years towards dyslexia in general. The LEA are regular attenders at our meetings of the local Dyslexia Association and we all co-operate very well together in trying to find solutions for children with dyslexic difficulties within Norfolk.

Did you seek help?

We contacted you, Bevé, at Bart's and although you were extremely busy you recognized our desperation and took Adrian on at your clinic on a weekly basis and under the caring teaching of dear Ann Lewey he did begin to make progress and more importantly began to have a belief in his abilities.

Was it successful?

We have today proved that all the blood, sweat and tears were absolutely worth it in that this afternoon Adrian discovered that he has achieved a degree in Business Administration and Finance, grade unknown as yet. He is intending to stay on for his honours next year. He is now 26 years old but he has proved to himself that he can be successful – even if it does take a few years longer. He has worked Saturdays and weekends as a cleaner at Burger King and we feel that he can be very proud of his efforts and perseverance. Needless to say both Mum and Dad and sister are delighted.

Did your child achieve any GCSEs, A levels, degrees?

Geography	History	Maths	Science	English	Design
C	C	C	C	D	B

History and Geography at 16
Science and Design at 17
Psychology A level evening class, Grade C at 21
Maths at 21
Business and finance HND
Business and finance degree

If he/she is now working, what job/career, profession is he/she following?

Adrian is still at Norwich City College.

Has he/she married?

Adrian is not married – no girlfriend but plenty of friends.

Any children?

Not as far as we know!

If so, are any dyslexic?

Adrian, I think, would agree that without the help of you and your staff he would certainly not be in the same position he is today. He used to say 'I know how other children read – I just can't make my brain do it'. From a very frightened little boy he has developed into a confident, articulate young man with a great sense of humour and a very caring attitude to others struggling as he has struggled.

As Adrian's mum I shall always be grateful for believing in us at a very demoralizing time in our lives.

Adrian's assessment

Department of Psychological Medicine
Dyslexia Clinic

Reply to referral letter
Dr J J Fox

1 November 1978

Dear Dr Fox:

Re: Master Adrian Fordham – 11.5.71

I saw the above little boy regarding his reading and writing difficulties on 27 October 1978 as requested. I first of all gave him a test of general intelligence, namely the Wechsler Intelligence Scale for Children 1949, on which he obtained the following results:

Verbal tests	Scaled score
Information	8
Comprehension	19
Arithmetic	9
Similarities	20
Vocabulary	19
(Digit span)	(8)

Performance tests	Scaled score
Picture completion	17
Picture arrangement	14
Block design	10
Object assembly	10
Coding	4

Where 10 is average and 20 maximum score. Later revisions give 19 as maximum score.

Verbal IQ	131
Performance IQ	107
Full scale IQ	121

This places Adrian in the superior range of intelligence but there is a considerable scatter on the subtest scores and a very significant discrepancy between the performance and verbal IQs of 24 points.

His particular weaknesses would seem to lie in visual sequencing and mental imagery for symbols (see coding). His verbal sequencing was also below average – digit span – which is a test requiring the subject to repeat numbers after the examiner, first in the same order that they are given and then in reverse order. Adrian was only able to repeat two numbers backwards.

Although reported to have no concept of number, his mental arithmetic was only marginally below average as was general information. On the other verbal subtests of comprehension, similarities and vocabulary he scored in the very superior range.

This is a little boy, then, with a very good intellectual level who is failing seriously in acquiring reading spelling and writing skills.

On the Neale Analysis of Reading Ability he made 10 errors on the first passage, which does give him a reading age of 6 years 10 months, but he could not be said to be really reading as he obtained no information from the material read and, indeed, it was largely incomprehensible. I think his difficulties would be best understood if I give you the passage as it is intended to be read and then Adrian's rendering of it.

Neale Passage One:

Father gave Pam a big box. Pam put it on the table. She looked in the box for a doll. Then out jumped a white rabbit.

Adrian read the following:

Frog gibs peg bit box. Peg buts it on the table. She lid in the box ron a dot. Then ont jumped a water rabbit.

Not surprisingly he was unable to answer any of the comprehension questions. Although Adrian has been taught some letter sounds (but not their names) he is quite unable to use these skills for phonic synthesis in reading and is largely guessing from the first letter of the word. He made some interesting mistakes in that he read 'n' for 'u' in the word 'out', 'b' for 'p' in the word 'puts' and reversed the order of letters as well as misreading them when he read 'ron' for 'for'.

On the Daniels and Diack Graded Word Spelling Test, Adrian had a spelling age of 6 years 2 months. Again he was able to spell totally phonetic three-letter words but was unable to appreciate consonant blends, thus writing 'los' for 'lost' and 'pan' for 'plan'. He also mirror wrote b, d and p. He is quite unable to write the alphabet but could write his numbers from 1 to 9.

On the Bender Gestalt (Koppitz Scoring) he scored at the 6½ year level, which is in line with his reading and spelling ages.

On the Wepman Auditory Discrimination Test he made two errors, which is within normal range for his age, involving the minimal pairs sheaf/sheath and them/then.

Adrian is right-handed and right-eyed but there is left-handedness in the family and he himself was late deciding which hand to use until the age of 5. He had always had difficulty in acquiring good pencil grip and is generally uncoordinated. All milestones were normal, including the onset of speech but he did have a severe speech defect, which has, to some extent, persisted.

Adrian Fordham receiving his degree.

He has always been a poor sleeper and finds it difficult to relax and this is reflected in his hyperactive behaviour. Adrian cannot tell the time and has no concept of time, not understanding in what order things are likely to happen in the day or, of course, in a year. He is not good at ball games and still has difficulty with stairs, though it is not quite understood whether this is a matter of vertigo or an artefact of his poor co-ordination. Indeed, it may well be a question of poor convergence for near vision and he does appear to have a mild strabismus. It is proposed to investigate this aspect of his vision. There are some minimal autistic touches such as perseveration, obsessive behaviour and hand wiggling but he is in no way autistic and these characteristics do often appear in the dyslexic.

Conclusions

In view of the above, I feel I can state that in our terms Adrian is dyslexic and requires very specialized help if he is to overcome his difficulties. With an IQ in the superior range he should be reading to two years above his chronological age rather than one year below. In addition, he has a cluster of typical signs and symptoms as already mentioned.

We have offered help at the Dyslexia Clinic on a once-a-week basis in the first instance but we do have a teacher who is doing the one-year teacher training course who lives in Norfolk and she may be able to take over the case when she completes the course in July 1979

Hoping that his attendance at the Clinic will be facilitated.

Yours sincerely,

Bevé Hornsby MSc, LCST (Mrs)

Head of Dyslexia Clinic

cc: Mr & Mrs Fordham

Dr G Harland, School Medical Officer

Norwich Community Health Partnership

NHS Trust

LEARNING DISABILITIES SERVICE

Little Plumstead Hospital, Norwich NR13 5EW
Tel (01603) 711 227   Safehaven Fax (01603) 711 202
E-Mail = krishnan@netcom.co.uk

Dr V H R Krishnan, Consultant Psychiatrist
Miss Sharon Blanch, Medical Secretary
Tel: (01603) 711 204 *(direct line)*

Our ref: VHRK/sjb/   Date: 18th December 1996

Mrs Hornsby
261 Trinity Road
LONDON SW18 3FN

Dear Mrs Hornsby

Adrian FORDHAM   Dob: 11.5.71
21 Malten Close, Poringland, Norwich NR14 7RW

Adrian, who is about 26 years of age, has recently begun attending my psychiatric outpatient clinic because of his severe anxiety related symptoms. I have taken permission from his parents to write to you.

I believe Adrian attended your special dyslexia clinic during your work at St Bartholomew's Hospital for about 2 years from around 1977 onwards. I am pleased to inform you that Adrian has indeed benefited from the Alpha to Omega method of approach and it is indeed my pleasure to report to you that Adrian's dyslexia at present is very minimal.

I have seen some of your reports to the child psychiatrists who were managing Adrian during the late 1970's and it would indeed be interesting to see if you have any other information about Adrian. I believe you are in the process of writing a book about Adrian and if you require any additional information please do not hesitate to write to me.

It would be helpful if you could send me some information about the Alpha to Omega approach and if there are any other publications relating to this approach could I please request you to let me have a copy of these publications.

Once again may I take this opportunity to let you know that Adrian is now functioning at a near normal level for his age and has ambitions to have a business of his own.

With regards,

Yours sincerely

[signature] 18/12/96.

Dr V H R Krishnan, MRCPsych, DPM
Consultant in Developmental Psychiatry

■ *Home Based Health Care* ■ *Community Hospitals* ■ *Health Promotion* ■ *Specialist Services* ■ **NHS**
2000

DR B. HORNSBY   MBE, PhD, MSc, MEd, FRCSLT, AFBPsS

Chartered Psychologist and Speech Therapist

10 Harley Street:
London WIN 1AA
Tel: 0171-436 5252
Fax: 0171-467 8312

Please reply to:
The Hornsby International
Dyslexia Centre
Glenshee Lodge
261 Trinity Road
London SW18 3SN
Tel: 0181-874 1844
Fax: 0181-877 9737
Private Fax: 0181-871 1092

Dr. V.H.R. Krishnan, MRCPsych, DPM
Consultant in Developmental Psychiatry
Norwich Community Health Partnership
Little Plumstead Hospital,
Norwich
NR13 5EW

2nd January 1997

Dear Dr. Krishnan,

re: **Adrian Fordham (d.o.b. 11.5.71)**

I was so delighted to receive your letter about Adrian. When I left Barts I was not able to take the files with me and it did not occur to me to collect addresses as I assumed I was retiring!

However, that has not proved to be the case and I am still going strong. I have managed to keep in touch with some of my Barts patients, but am also very pleased to have news of them.

Now that I am writing a book to be called "Dyslexics I have known", it becomes more and more vital that I should know as much as possible about them. I would, therefore, be grateful for anything you could send me that would be of interest.

I enclose our Resource List - all the workbooks relate to the programme Alpha to Omega. Also enclosed is a leaflet on teaching and a copy of my book 'Overcoming Dyslexia'.

If there is anything further you would like, please let me know.

May I take this opportunity to send you good wishes for the New Year.

Yours sincerely,

Bevé Hornsby

John Andrews

An unsolicited testimonial also showing that mature adults can be helped by specialist tuition.

Dear Dr Hornsby
I have just finished reading *Overcoming Dyslexia* and I felt I had to write to tell you how thankful I am to you and your dedicated teachers.

My husband is dyslexic. He was struggling at work and his self-esteem was at rock bottom. After some tests at work, John was sick with worry. I spent two entire days phoning around for help. I phoned the British Dyslexia Association, the Dyslexia Institute and advice lines in Salisbury and Southampton. All that my calls achieved was increased frustration and only added to our despair. One of the helpers on the advice line even told me my husband was more likely to be stupid than dyslexic.

We weren't getting any sensible answers and a couple of the people we encountered really spoke down to us. They promised to ring back but never did so. Helpful they were not. Then through a friend we heard of Tina Jubb who has been like a breath of fresh air. As soon as she stepped in we felt a great weight lift from our shoulders. Nothing seemed so bad because Tina is always so positive.

So far John has had six lessons and I have seen him change before my eyes. His reading and spelling have improved but it is far more than that. John is reading books, writing letters, and is being promoted at work. He is happier and more confident than I have ever known him and hoping to start an HND when he finishes with Tina.

There is no doubting in our minds that Tina is magic. She advised us to read your books and I've since discovered that she trained under you. We also have *Alpha to Omega* so that I can help John at home.

A big thanks so much for teachers like Tina and for your books.

Yours sincerely
Margaret Andrews

The heritability of dyslexia

A delightfully dyslexic family!

The father, Dr David Mathias, is a GP and his dyslexia was picked up at Great Ormond Street Hospital when he took his second eldest son, Michael, to be assessed. So many doctors seem to be dyslexic that I wonder if that is why their prescriptions are virtually illegible!

Mrs Marilyn Mathias, the mother of this enchanting family, has a father who is ambidextrous, so presumably he would have been left-handed if not interfered with at school. She, herself, has dyscalculia (trouble with maths) and considerable directional confusion.

They have three sons, Andrew, Michael and Tom, all of whom are dyslexic.

Andrew is now 35 and is married with two children, a boy and a girl. William has been diagnosed dyslexic. Katie, being a girl, is less affected but nevertheless needs watching, Mrs Mathias thinks. In spite of everything, Andrew has overcome his problems to a large extent and is now a lawyer.

Michael is 32 and left-handed as well as dyslexic. He is married, but has no children as yet. He went to Hurstpierpoint School and managed seven O levels and two A levels, but with poor grades.

Tom is 23 and not yet married. He would like to take up teaching dyslexics and is considering doing a course.

Bill Thomson

Mr Bill Thomson, aged 54, is dyslexic and learnt to read and write only when he discovered yellow paper and red ink! Bill has won many awards and was UK runner up in the Senior Learner of the Year award for 1998, organized by The National Organization for Adult Learning (NIACE).

New life for man who couldn't read

A 54-YEAR-OLD man, who until recently couldn't read or write, is now an author of short stories and poetry.

Bill Thomson, of Bruce Road, Glenrothes, had simply accepted his difficulties — until his daughter put some colour into his life and turned it round completely.

"I always knew I was different when I was at school," admits Bill. "But my mother and father, a shepherd, never ever said I was stupid and sacrificed a lot for me.

"They paid for my bus fares off farm wages to go to Markinch School a few miles away, where I was in a remedial class. I should have gone to a school nearby, which my brother attended.

"I worked as a gardener when I left school and did manual work in a paper mill because I couldn't read or write.

"I was often in tears through my adult years, as the work was difficult and I was very frustrated."

Bill married in 1971 and he and his wife, June, now have a 15-year-old daughter Leanne.

It was when Leanne asked Bill how to spell a word that he decided to start learning classes. He says simply, "It was something wonderful that was to turn my world upside down."

Because when Bill attended classes at Glenrothes College, they discovered that not only was he dyslexic, but he suffered from a rare colour disorder that put words out of focus.

"Christine Proctor at the college found I had scotopic sensitivity syndrome. White paper and blue or black ink disorientated my eyes, but a yellow overlay suddenly brings everything into focus."

Yellow paper

Bill can now read books and even write poetry and short stories.

He still can't write with black or blue ink on white paper. Instead, he uses yellow paper and writes with pink-coloured ink.

His progress since his amazing problem was diagnosed has been so dramatic that he has won major awards. He's been named Scottish Television's Adult Learner of the Year and runner-up in the 1998 UK National Learner of the Year Awards.

Bill puts it all down to Christine and his teacher Bert Hughes — and to daughter Leanne who brought his life back into focus.

■ Bill showing off his new skills to daughter Leanne.

Courtesy of The Sunday Post and reporter Colin Macfarlane 31 May 1998

I'm different – I'm dyslexic

Not being able to read or write
Can lead to depression and misery.
Thank goodness others have seen the light
And given us hope and the energy.

To pull us out of this endless spiral
Of diminishing confidence.
These people to me are special,
For here I have the evidence

Right here in my hands.
From off white paper I cannot read,
My eyes hurt, to let you understand,
But when I cover this over with my yellow optic sheet

There is a world of words I've never seen before.
Now I can learn and it's more information that I seek.
No more will my mind be a closed door.
This is why I'm runner-up in the UK's over fifties week.

© Bill Thomson

I read this poem out at the United Kingdom awards in Leeds. I came runner-up out of 210 entries.

Alison Fenwick's story

As the patients seen at Bart's were of all ages and were suffering from a multiplicity of learning problems, I felt it important to include Alison to show how the same multisensory structured, dyslexia-oriented teaching could work with all children, no matter what the nature of their problems.

Alison and her sister Beverley were born in Nottingham on 7 June 1963, a pair of conjoined (Siamese) twins joined at the top of their heads, so sharing one skull with complete bone union. They were delivered by Caesarean section and were transferred to Bart's when they were two weeks old, with a view to separation at a future date. They were delightful babies, always content, presumably because they had each other all the time. Their surgery was dependent on a long and complicated series of investigations, which took a year to complete, but which were vital if there was to be any hope of final separation. It was found that the babies shared all the main cerebral vessels, including the circulation of cerebrospinal fluid. Eventually, after a year, the separation was attempted – this was extensive, difficult and seemingly impossible surgery. The separation took nearly 20 hours and, sadly, Beverley died in theatre, but somehow, miraculously, Alison survived.

She made slow but steady progress following the surgery and learned to sit up and move around freely, which she had never been able to do pre-separation. But she did have a left side paresis and obvious signs of serious brain damage. Her leg recovered but she still has a weak hand. Alison went home when she was two years old, walking, talking and playing, and much loved by all staff. Later she went to a school for disabled children near her home. She enjoyed school but had learning difficulties, as she is partially sighted and had problems similar to those of dyslexic children. Eventually at 13 it was realized that she needed (and deserved) special help and she came back to Bart's to be assessed by Mrs Hornsby, who said she would like to try and help her. She loved her lessons with Mrs Hornsby, which were always a time for fun and laughter, and, slowly, Alison learnt to read and write. She also attended a school in London for disabled children and left at 16 to start working in the sterilizing department at Bart's where she proudly packed instruments and dressings.

Sadly, about five years ago, she had a severe fall down a flight of marble stairs, and following that her problems returned and her reading ability was severely impaired again. At this time it was suggested to her that maybe she might try to paint using an easel on a table and looking straight ahead. If she turned her head from side to side her balance became badly affected.

Alison is a delightful and persevering young lady who never gives up. She has learned to paint in oils and has achieved much through her own determination. Her paintings are printed ink greetings cards and notelets, which are sold in the League of Friends shop at Bart's, and which are very popular with patients, visitors, staff and also with her many friends. She is a marvellous example of survival against all the odds and she will always be grateful to Mrs Hornsby (whom she loves dearly) for giving her the chance to prove that she was not 'just stupid'.

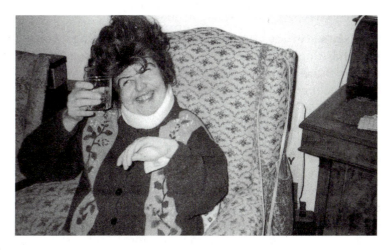

Alison

Sister H Clark, 1 December 1998

Sister 'Kenton' (as she was affectionately known because the children's ward was called Kenton) looked after Alison from the moment she was born and throughout her constant visits to Bart's, where she underwent many subsequent operations and treatment. Sister eventually adopted Alison and they have lived together ever since, coming to London regularly to attend the Bart's Guild functions where I see them both. Alison is now 36 and still going strong.

Craig Tomkins

Please return to: Dr Bevé Hornsby, The Hornsby Centre, 261 Trinity Rd, London SW18 3SN

Questionnaire for parents

Name: Margaret Tomkins
Name/names of child/children: Craig Tomkins

Please answer the following questions as fully as possible, making amusing or anecdotal comments wherever appropriate.

Was it a relief when your child was diagnosed dyslexic?

Yes it was a total relief. Craig struggled so much and hated his school day. At the age of 5 Craig said 'Mum chop me up and put me in the dustbin, I'm useless, I cannot do the things that other children can do'. Craig was diagnosed dyslexic at the age of 7, as I believed that was the magic age. I have since learnt that Craig could have been diagnosed earlier.

Did anybody's attitude change? Child, school, siblings, yourself?

Yes everybody's attitude changed. Craig was offered an assessment by the headteacher of the school he was attending, which was too late in the day! My attitude changed. I became understanding towards Craig's problem offering him the support he needed.

Did you seek help?

Yes immediately, I found Hornsby House School and took Craig for an interview. Craig was luckily offered a place and he started his new school within 2 days, receiving the help he so needed. When he left Hornsby House School at the age of 11 Craig was very sad but he went on to Mark College in Somerset as a boarder and was equally happy. Craig now boards at St Bede's School, where he is in the sixth form, and is still supported by special needs.

Was it successful?
Absolutely successful, Craig's attitude and behaviour changed immediately. At long last Craig was enjoying his school day, as his needs were being totally met. He made friends and became a more confident person. He was very happy and achieving.

Did your child achieve any GCSEs, A levels, degrees?
Craig achieved 7 GCSEs, 3 Bs, 3 Cs and 1 D grade in English language. He has recently retaken the GCSE exam again because he was not satisfied with the grade awarded. What determination! He is currently studying A-level media studies and GNVQ business studies and has already made his mind up to go on to university to do a degree.

If he/she is now working, what job/career, profession is he/she following?
N/A

Has he/she married?
No.

Any children?
No.

If so, are any dyslexic?
N/A

Is your son/daughter:

Left-handed: Yes/No   No

Crossed lateral: Yes/No   I would say yes, he writes with his right
                                hand but kicks a football with his left foot!

(left-handed but right-eyed or right-handed and left-eyed). If you are not sure about your preferred eye, make a small hole in an A4 size paper, hold the paper in both hands, take it close to your face and look at something through the hole. Note which eye is used.

Is there any family history of left-handedness?   Yes/No   Yes

David Shaw

David (date of birth 18.8.65) was one of the pupils treated at Bart's Hospital Dyslexia Clinic, and is now 34 years of age. He was not assessed at Bart's as there was such a long waiting list. His assessment was carried out privately,

Year 8 Architecture Project

Christopher Whitefield

Craig Tomkins

Simon Webb

Entries for the Dyslexia Institute's 'As I See It' competition

at the age of eight years and seven months. He was found to be of average intelligence, but a non-starter in reading and spelling.

David subsequently came to Bart's where I taught him for two years and he eventually passed eight CSEs at grades 3, 4 and 5.

David wanted to do computer studies, but was not allowed to as he was not in the class that was studying for O-level maths; this in spite of the fact that he was brilliant at computers and science. David can understand how anything works, with or without the instruction manual!

He eventually passed the City and Guilds Certificates Parts I and II in electronic systems and industrial equipment with distinction in 1984, while studying at DeHavilland College, Boreham Wood.

For the past nine years, David has worked for Mercury Communications (now Cable and Wireless) as an estates surveyor, helping to plan telephone installations in commercial buildings and negotiating with landlords and land owners for the granting of wayleaves, easements, etc.

His mother says David is a well-adjusted young man. He has his own flat and runs a Tenant's Association. He has a wide circle of friends, is interested in charity and social work, is capable and self-sufficient, and has a wide vocabulary.

Obviously, the computer age has helped him enormously, but his mother feels that the help David received at Bart's was the opening of a door for him in the early years.

Both his mother and father are enormously proud of David's achievements, as can be imagined.

There is no doubt that sound, dyslexia-orientated teaching at the earliest possible moment is the key to eventual success, both at school and in future adult life.

David being taught with his mother watching.

David as an adult.

Dyslexic reading upside down

My dear Dr Hornsby,

We spoke today about my grandson who, without any prior notice, read two or three lines from *Dark Knights and Dingy Castles* upside down. It was a question-and-answer page with the answers written upside down. I was reading to him and suddenly he chipped in with the answer more fluently than he reads right way up! I asked him if he had read upside down before. He said 'no, never' and that was that; end of subject!

I have since been having a go myself and find I can read upside down almost as fast as right way up. As I mentioned, I learnt to add up shopping bills upside down before the advent of checkout tills, and still do in small retail outlets, where appropriate.

It was greatly enjoyable talking with you. So interesting to learn about Per Udden and his reference to upside-down reading.

By the way another trick I have is to write without looking at what I am writing. So, taking information down off a blackboard for example does not need the redirecting of the eyes. Useful when needing to give gas, electric, etc., numbers on the back of cheques. Just look at numbers and write them without looking at the handwriting.

Sincerely
Irene Dodds.

Dr Per Udden, the founder of the Rodin Remediation Academy, certainly proposed the theory that dyslexics would fare better if they were exposed to upside-down print. Maybe this is so for some, but since this is not what one encounters in everyday life, the idea was not pursued. Bernard Shaw's 'Simplified Spelling' would probably have suffered a similar fate, but for the fact that he left his entire fortune to the Simplified Spelling Society, which is still in existence.

I do not think the new alphabet devised by academics at Salford University, which they have called TOMAXAMOT because it is a palindrome and each letter is symmetrical, will succeed either. The example of this new alphabet published in the *Times Educational Supplement* of 4 September 1998 is, in my opinion, likely to meet the same fate.

Further reading

Cooke A (1999) *Memories of the Great and the Good*. London: Pavilion Books.
Udden P (1999) The Rodin Remediation Academy, POB 1303, CH-6061, Sarnen, Switzerland.

3 Apex Lodge
35 Lyonsdown Road
New Barnet, Herts.

12th September, 1984

Mrs. Beve Hornsby, Dyslexia Dept
c/o St Bartholmews Hospital
London E.C.1.

Dear Mrs. Hornsby

I thought you might be interested to know about t6he progress of my Son
David Shaw who was lucky enough to be one of your pupils at the Dyslexia
Clinic during the mid Seventies.

He is now nineteen and after spending two years at DeHavilland College
studing for a City and Guilds Certificate in Electronic Servicing he has
passed his Part I with Distinction and Credit and Part II with three
Credits. Copy Certificate enclosed.

I might add that out of 24 boys who started the course in 1983 David and
two other boys were the only ones to pass Part II.

If it were not for you and your Dept opening the door for him this would
have never been possible. Again our very grateful thanks.

Hoping that you are keeping well.

With kindest regards.

Yours sincerely,

Jacqueline Shaw

Jacqueline Shaw.

Warman-Johnston S (1998) Department of Professional Studies, Salford University.
Times Educational Supplement 4th September 1998.

Tomaxamot translation:
The text says
'This is Tamaxamot, a
character set which is
mirror reflective. Inversible
palindromic.'

Synaesthesia

A lady I met on a cruise, Dorothy Anderson, told me that she recognizes words by their colour, and she subsequently sent me several articles relating to the subject. Synaesthesia, like dyslexia, comes from the Greek – syn (union), aisthesis (sensation) – and means that stimulation in one modality (sense organ) gives rise to an experience in another.

This condition has been known to the scientific community for nearly 300 years and yet has remained relatively unexplored. There are many accounts of the condition impacting upon the fields of art, music and literature. Rimsky-Korsakov is said to have had synaesthesia, which gave him a feeling of colour when certain notes were played, and Scriabin also experienced odour. Liszt's synaesthesia is reported to have invaded the conducting of his orchestral pieces when he would say 'more pink here, if you please' or 'more orange there'.

Baudelaire's 'Correspondences' suggests that he believed there was a natural correspondence between the senses.

A contemporary author – Andrea Newman – used colour a great deal in her selection of words. Thus, when faced with a choice of words such as 'confused' or 'bewildered', she would select the one whose colour fitted best with the colour of the other words in the sentence. Apparently some synaesthetists perceive single letters in colour, which relates to the first letter of a word so that if 'p' was blue, pound, pig and penny would all appear blue, whereas others see whole words as variations of different colours. According to the importance of the word in the reader's mind, the stronger the colour. For example 'pound' might be almost purple whereas 'penny' would be an insipid, wishy-washy blue!

To ascertain which subjects had synaesthesia and which not, many experiments have been carried out, but the one with the most positive results is being conducted by Paulesu, Harrison, Baron-Cohen, Watson, Frith, Goldstein and Frankowiak (1998) in Cambridge, using positron emission tomography (PET) scans. They predicted that the synaesthetists would show increased blood flow to certain areas of the brain that detect colour when shown words, which was not the case with the control group. Further research is being carried out by them to see if the colours are first related to phonemes in non-readers and later to letters when they have learnt to read.

Perhaps these experiments may add another dimension to the multisensory teaching techniques used with dyslexics. If they are synaesthetic, they might find the use of colour to help memorize spelling patterns a powerful mnemonic. For example, if 'fight' is associated with war, the 'ight' might be given (or chosen) as the colour red, or the 'ee' in 'tree' as 'green' and 'ea' in 'sea' as 'blue'. Who knows, it is worth a try!

Further reading

Cytowic RE (1993) *The Man who Tasted Shapes*. New York: Putnam.

Luria A (1968) *The Mind of a Mnemonist*. New York: Basic Books.

Myers C (1914) A case of synaesthesia. *British Journal of Psychology* : 228–238.

Paulesu E, Harrison J, Baren-Cohen S, Watson J, Frith C, Frankowiak RSJ (2000). *The Functional Anatomy of Synaesthesia* (in press).

Wells A (1980) Music and visual colour; a proposed correlation. *Leonardo* **13**: 100.

CHAPTER 13

Statistical results

It can be seen from the figures below that the preponderance of passes at A and B grades for dyslexic pupils with IQs in range 122 to 129 (superior) does not differ significantly from that of dyslexic pupils with IQs of 130+ (very superior), although gifted children with IQs of over 146 do fare better with regard to A-level grades overall.

This must surely indicate that individuals with IQs of 125+ stand as good a chance of obtaining good grades as their supposedly brighter peers, presumably because other factors are influencing the outcome, such as motivation, parental expectation, confidence in oneself, ability to concentrate and so on.

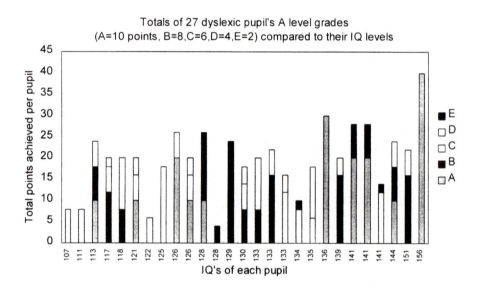

Figure 13.1: Totals of 27 dyslexic pupils' A-level grades.

Of course, it must be borne in mind that these results apply only to children whose parents were able to afford the initial assessment, obtain appropriate specialist help and obtain extra time concessions in their examinations. This does not mean that they all came from a high socioeconomic class, as all social classes are represented, as in the normal distribution curve both at Bart's Hospital, where the assessments and treatment were on the NHS and at the Centre, which is fee-paying. Nevertheless, a considerable proportion of patients/clients had obviously made enormous efforts to obtain the necessary fees (usually produced in cash from their back pocket!) or had benefited from our bursary fund. And they must have been caring parents to take so much trouble to ensure their children received the right kind of help.

Further statistical results

On the question of heritability or family history of dyslexia, the figure of 80% has been arrived at in a number of studies. Indeed, in my own PhD study involving the patients at Bart's Hospital the figure was 88%. The results are now published in *Overcoming Dyslexia* (Hornsby 1997). An article that appeared in *New Scientist* in August 1994 really sums up the question of genes and their relevance to dyslexia. To quote:

Dyslexia gene lurks in chromosome's 'black hole'

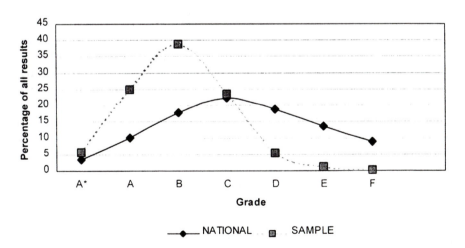

GCSE results for 60 dyslexic pupils compared to the 1996 National GCSE results

Figure 13.2: GCSE results of 60 dyslexic pupils compared with the national average.

Total of 60 dyslexic pupils' GCSE grades (A = 10 points, B = 8, C = 6, D = 4, E = 2) on top of their IQs

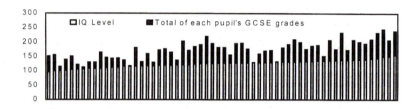

Figure 13.3: Total of 60 dyslexic pupils' GCSE grades on top of their IQs

Total of 27 dyslexic pupils' A level grades (A = 10 points, B = 8, C = 6, D = 4, E = 2) on top of their IQs

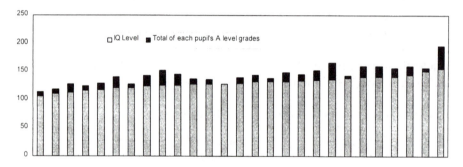

Figure 13.4: Total of 27 dyslexic pupils' A-level grades on top of their IQs.

Dyslexia is known to run in families. But just how much of it is inherited and which genes are responsible are as yet not fully known, although American researchers now claim to have mapped a key genetic factor to a region on chromosome 6.

The disorder, which affects between 5 and 10 per cent of schoolchildren, is diagnosed on the basis of a child's failure to achieve a target score in reading tests. The causes of dyslexia are highly complex, and involve a host of genetic and environmental factors, says Lon Cardon of the Department of Mathematics at Stanford University in California (*Science*, 22 October, 1994 p 276).

To find all the genes that contribute to dyslexia would involve searching through the whole human genome for correspondence, or 'linkage', between reading disability and the inheritance of particular genetic sequences. Cardon and his colleagues narrowed the search by exploiting the known association between the genes involved in autoimmune diseases such as migraine and

A level results for 27 dyslexic pupils

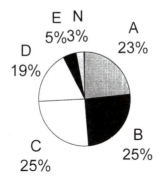

Figure 13.5: A-level results for 27 dyslexic pupils in percentages.

Sample of 87 dylexic people with a family history of dyslexia

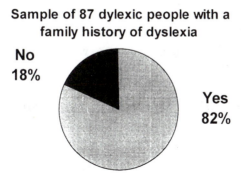

Figure 13.6: Sample of 87 dyslexic people with a family history of dyslexia.

asthma, and those responsible for dyslexia. Autoimmune diseases are more common in people with dyslexia, and in their relatives.

Cardon and his team studied 179 sibling pairs and 50 sets of non-identical twins, one of whom had been diagnosed as dyslexic in each case. They looked for correspondences between low reading scores and the inheritance of specific genetic sequences in the part of chromosome 6 known as the human leukocyte antigen region. The HLA region is known to have a role in autoimmune diseases.

Using a statistical technique that they developed themselves, the researchers found a high linkage between reading disability and sequences in the HLA region in the sibling pairs, which they then confirmed in the twins. The more extreme the reading deficits, the stronger the linkage they found.

This quantitative approach is a powerful one, says Robert Plomin, a behavioural scientist at the Institute of Psychiatry in London. 'The fact that they have replicated their results is very impressive,' he says.

But Plomin warns: 'They have only identified a chromosomal region, not a gene for reading disability.' He describes the HLA region as the 'black hole of molecular genetics', because it could involve a large number of genes.

Cardon claims to have isolated a narrow stretch within that complex. This area could harbour anywhere between 30 and 100 genes, 'which is a pretty tight linkage,' he says. Other regions on other chromosomes probably play a part too, but the researchers believe they are close to finding one of the prominent genes in dyslexia. Once they do, it could play a major role in early diagnosis and intervention.

Spinney L (1994) *New Scientist* 22 October, 1994.

In the present study the figure was 82%, which suggests that 80% plus or minus eight is a reliable figure.

Assessment results for dyslexic people

- Average verbal intelligence quotient: 124
- Average performance intelligence quotient: 118
- Average full scale intelligence quotient: 124

It is interesting to note that in spite of the fact that 80% of dyslexics were latish to very late on speech or language development, the overall average IQ on the verbal scale is higher than that of the performance or visuo-spatial IQ. This could, of course, be explained by the fact that the perform-ance items require not only the ability to solve visually presented problems, but also manual dexterity, as all items are timed. Many dyslexics are dyspraxic (clumsy) and this militates against their obtaining top scores on these tasks.

Regarding the question of left-handedness and crossed laterality, the results are not significant (see Figures 13.7 and 13.8).

**Incidence of crossed laterality in
sample of 98 dyslexic people**

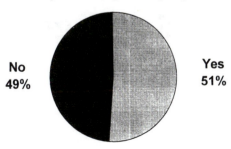

No
49%

Yes
51%

Figure 13.7: Incidence of crossed laterality in 98 dyslexics.

Left-handedness in a sample of 107 dyslexic people

Yes
21%

No
79%

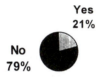

Figure 13.8: Incidence of left-handedness in 107 dyslexics.

Reference

Hornsby B (1997) *Overcoming Dyslexia: a straightforward guide for families and teachers*. London: Random House.

CHAPTER 14

So where do we go from here?

'Teacher training still inadequate says a second report by the Office for Standards in Education (OFSTED) which confirms that by the end of their four year teacher training course, students at most teacher training colleges have not learnt how to teach reading; Nor do they have a secure grasp of the subject knowledge of English. What chance of higher standards in schools until ALL teachers are properly trained?

YOU CANNOT TEACH WHAT YOU DO NOT KNOW.'

Jean Chall (1967) says we need to find ways in which teachers can be trained in phonetics and linguistics and beginning reading skills. Teachers need to know why they should acquire this knowledge and how to make best use of it. They need to know the history of reading instruction, for in reading, as in other aspects of life, those who ignore history are likely to repeat its errors.

It is a pity she makes the same mistake that so many academics do – that is, she refers to reading only, whereas literacy requires good spelling, well-formed handwriting which can be read and logically presented material which can easily be understood. I would like to finish with a quote from Her Majesty's Chief Inspector, presented in the spring 1998 issue of the *Newsletter of the Campaign for Real Education.*

Conclusion

Ladies and gentlemen, one key lesson of educational reform is that the state cannot mandate educational excellence by top down regulation. It is at least arguable that reforms do not so much change schools as schools change reforms; it is obvious that it is only the teacher who can ensure that standards rise. Hence my emphasis tonight on the factors which have the greatest influence on the quality of teaching. Can the state do more to solve the problem I have not yet touched upon, the problem which some would allege to be the most serious of all: namely, low morale? I do not in fact believe that the profession is nearly as

108

demoralised as some would have us believe. If you are a Union Leader you have an obvious reason to emphasise difficulties with morale; so, too, if you are opposed to the drive to render the profession accountable. It is not the ritual humiliation of teachers across the country that explains low morale, for the situation is radically different in one school from another. In my experience, demoralised teachers are to be found in schools where headteachers find it easier to blame the inspectorate, the Government and the media than to confront problems which they could and should have dealt with themselves, in schools where the head is unable to prioritise, cannot see the wood from the trees, has neither the intellectual capacity to chart the way forward nor the authority to carry others with him. This is not, of course, to suggest that the inspectorate, the Government and the media cannot through their actions raise or depress morale. OFSTED, for its part, whilst continuing as we must to speak out bluntly whenever inspectors find under-achievement, will do all it can to ensure that good teachers and schools receive the credit they so richly deserve. Doug McAvoy might find this divisive and elitist; I am not prepared to pretend that everyone is doing a similarly effective job and I believe that any such pretence would in fact undermine the morale of those who know they are working harder and more effectively and achieving better results than their peers. The Government should do two things. It ought, first, to ensure that the context in which teachers teach makes the best possible professional sense: that the curriculum is both teachable and intellectually demanding; that in-service training is relevant and available; that every possible penny of resourcing reaches the classroom. And, second, it must resist the temptation to do too much too quickly. Schools can only do so much at once and primary schools, in particular, need time to devote themselves to implementing the literacy and numeracy strategies.

Then morale is down to the profession. When teachers teach better they will have greater public esteem and their morale will as a consequence be higher. It is a hard thing, moreover, to say but the profession, in my judgement, does itself no favours if it pretends to hold the monopoly on stress and pressure. 'If', a friend outside education said to me a month or so ago, 'I hear another teacher whinging on about how stressed they are, I shall scream.' Teaching is, of course, stressful in very particular ways, but other jobs do have their moments. If the profession could bring itself to talk up the delights and satisfactions of teaching as a career it would do itself an enormous good – and it might help with the problem of recruitment, too.

Indeed, the last moral I want to draw tonight is that if Government is able to achieve less than it might want to believe, those who speak on behalf of teachers could achieve an awful lot more. There are honourable exceptions (in which category, of course, I would include the many luminaries I see before me), but so much of what is written about teachers and teaching is either negative in the way it harks on about the awfulness of the job or intellectually dubious in the vision it purports to articulate. It is the latter that worries me most because, as I have emphasised, if our concept of education is wrong then nothing much is likely to happen. Delaying the moment on Sunday when I had to start thinking about this lecture, I browsed through the *Observer*. My gaze alighted on an article on the 'post-millennium classroom', which is, I have to confess, exactly the sort of phrase that sends shivers down my spine. The shivers intensified as I read on. We ought apparently: 'to look back on what we were taught in colleges of education from the bible of one Michael (sic) Hirst, who wrote that teaching was about transmitting essential knowledge from one generation to the next.' We now know better. We now know that learning does not work like that, 'far from thinking coming after knowledge, knowledge comes on the coat-tails of thinking ... therefore instead of knowledge-centred schools we need thinking-centred schools.' Oh dear! This is a Professor of Education who does not even know that Professor Hirst's christian name is Paul, not Michael, and who dismissed with contemptuous indifference the idea that education is about teaching the young and ignorant things that they need to know **if they are to grow a little wiser**. But, what really depresses me is the intellectual shoddiness of the argument. Whoever thought that 'thinking came after knowledge'? Nothing new and difficult is ever learnt without serious intellectual effort. This verges on the tautologous. How can 'thinking skills' or any of those other qualities 'so prized by employers – communication skills, self-confidence, self presentation, problem solving, teamwork, independent thinking, breadth of interest, capacity for learning' be taught in a knowledge vacuum?

I'll let this stand as a rhetorical question. This article is a classic example of how down on the bedrock the crusade for higher standards involves a clash of ideologies which will be resolved not by the intrusion of political will but by the exercise of a quality which is in rather short supply: intellectual clarity. It is on that rather bleak note, ladies and gentlemen, that I will end and invite comments and discussion.

I think that says it all.

For a copy of the full speech please send an A5 stamped addressed envelope to:

Nick Seaton, Chairman, Campaign for Real Education, 18 Westlands Grove, Stockton Lane, York YO3 OEF.

References:

Chall J (1967) *Learning to Read – the great debate*. New York: McGraw-Hill.
Newsletter of the Campaign for Real Education (1998) **12**(1).

International phonetic alphabet

PHONETIC SYMBOLS FOR ENGLISH TRANSCRIPTION

CONSONANTS

/ p / pop	/ f / fife	/ m / mime
/ b / bib	/ v / verve	/ n / nine
/ t / tot	/ θ / thigh	/ ŋ / singing
/ d / did	/ ð / they	/ l / loyal
/ k / kick	/ s / cease	/ r / rarer
/ g / gag	/ z / zoos	/ j / yo-yo
/ tʃ / church	/ ʃ / shush	/ w / wayward
/ dʒ / judge	/ ʒ / treasure	/ h / how

VOWELS

/ iː / peat	/ uː / fool	/ ʊə / Ruhr
/ ɪ / pit	/ ɜː / bird	/ ə / banana
/ e / pet	/ eɪ / fail	/ æ / pat
/ əʊ / foal	/ ʌ / bud	/ aɪ / file
/ ɑː / bard	/ aʊ / foul	/ ɒ / pot
/ ɔɪ / foil	/ ɔː / port	/ ɪə / pier
/ ʊ / put	/ ɛə / pear	

111

Schools grading system

UK system	American system	
Key stage 1 covers 1st and 2nd years of school – ages 5–6	Grade I	6 years
	Grade II	7 years
Key stage 2 covers 3rd–6th years of school – ages 7–11	Grade III	8 years
	Grade IV	9 years
Key stage 3 covers 7th–9th years of school – ages 12–14	Grade V	10 years
	Grade VI	11 years
Key stage 4 covers 10th and 11th years of school – ages 15–16 years	Grade VII	12 years
	Grade VIII	13 years
	Grade IX	14 years
	Grade X	15 years
Key stage 1 covers Levels 1–3	Grade XI	16 years
Key stage 2 covers Levels 2–5	Grade XII	17 years
Key stage 3 covers Levels 3–7	Grade XIII	18 years
Key stage 4 covers Levels 4–10	(first year at college)	

APPENDIX 3

The speech audiogram

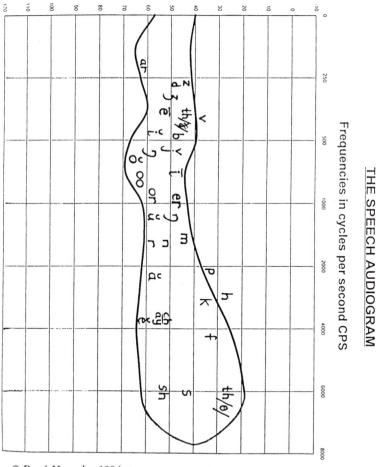

Sound intensity in decibles

© Bevé Hornsby 1994

113

Categories of IQ test scores and examination predictions

The British Psychological Society has recommended the following descriptive categories of IQ test scores:

69 and below	intellectually deficient
70–79	borderline
80–119	average
	80–89 low average
	90–109 average
	110–119 high average
120–129	superior
130+	very superior.

For purposes of comparison, the following IQ figures relate to examination or grade potential:

90+	GCSE
118+	A level
120+	university degree or professional qualification.

Source: Hernstein RJ, Murray C (1994) *The Bell Curve: Intelligence and class structure in American life*. The Free Press.

Example of Initial Teaching Alphabet (ITA), 1960

tradiʃhonally wun ov ʃhe first tasks ov ʃhe infant scω͡l woʒ tω teeɥ ɥildren tω reeɖ. it iʒ still, kwiet rietly, a mæjor pre-occuepæʃhon, sins reeɖiŋ iʒ a kee tω muɥ ov ʃhe leɼniŋ ʃhat will cum læter anɖ tω ʃhe possibility ov inɖepenɖent study. in meny infant scω͡lʒ, reeɖiŋ anɖ rietiŋ aɼ treeteɖ aʒ ekstenʃhonʒ ov spœken laŋgwæj. ʃhœʒ ɥildren hω͡ hav not haɖ ʃhe opportuenïity at·hœm tω grasp ʃhe paɼt ʃhat ʃhæ plæ aɼ introɖuest tω ʃhem bie ʃhe everydæ events anɖ envieronment ov ʃhe classrω͡m. messæjeʒ tω gœ hœm, letterʒ tω sick ɥildren, læbelʒ tω enʃhuer ʃhat mateerialʒ anɖ tω͡lʒ aɼ returnɖ tω ʃhæɼ proper plæʒ; aull caull for reeɖiŋ anɖ rietiŋ. meny ɥildren first glimps ʃhe pleʒuerʒ ov reeɖiŋ from liseniŋ tω storiʒ reɖ tω ʃhem at scω͡l. . . . bω͡ks mæɖ bie teeɥerʒ anɖ ɥildren about ʃhe ɖω͡iŋʒ ov ʃhe class or ov indiviɖuealʒ in it figuer prominently amuŋ ʃhe bω͡ks whiɥ ɥildren enjoi. ʃhæ help ɥildren tω see meeniŋ in reeɖiŋ anɖ tω appreeʃhiæt ʃhe puɼpos ov ritten recorɖʒ.

115

Professor Malarky, an odd ode

In the days of his boyhood, Professor Malarky
Spoke simply and clearly and knew how to spell,
But as he grew older he pondered this question:
'Why couldn't everyone do so as well ?'
So he studied dyslexia, also dyslalia,
Linguistics as well – and his knowledge increased,
And he found to his joy that the world of phonetics
Provided a terminological feast!
How seductive were phonemes and morphemes and graphemes
And fricative uvulars, allophones too!
He exulted whenever a plosive was glottal
And never used short words when long ones would do!
Soon he was practising phatic communion
With Alexia (this was the name of his cat)
But she merely made nasal bilabial noises
So he made a phonetic transcription of that!
Gone were the days when he used to think SYNTAX
Was something that sinners must pay when they sinned –
Now he was sailing the Sea of Semantics,
Breasting the waves with his sails full of wind!
Prolific indeed were the deeps of this ocean
With affricates, laterials, nasals and rolls
And he learnt all the hundreds of sounds that they made,
For these curious creatures abounded in shoals!
At last they awarded Professor Malarky
The Chair of Phonetics at Frinton-on-Sea,
Where he lectured on morphophonemic components
And other such matters beyond you and me.
The students attending his lectures were happy
To sit at the feet of a Master, no doubt
Though some of them said they'd be happier still
If they knew what on earth he was talking about!

© David Hornsby

Index